THE TOP 100

Coffee

RECIPES

A COOKBOOK
FOR COFFEE DRINKERS

THE TOP 100

RECIPES

A COOKBOOK
FOR COFFEE DRINKERS

MARY WARD

PHOTOGRAPHY BY BARNEY TAXEL

WINGS BOOKS
NEW YORK • AVENEL, NEW JERSEY

This 1995 edition is published by Wings Books, distributed by Random House Value Publishing, Inc., 40 Engelhard Avenue, Avenel, New Jersey 07001, by arrangement with Lifetime Books, Inc.

Prop/food stylist: Mary Ward
Photographer: Barney Taxel
Introduction: Timothy J. Castle

Random House
New York • Toronto • London • Sydney • Auckland

Printed and bound in the United States of America

Library of Congress Cataloging–in–Publication Data
Ward, Mary, 1940–
    The top 100 coffee recipes : a cookbook for coffee drinkers / by Mary Ward.
        p.   cm.
    Includes index.
    ISBN 0–517–14713–0   (hardcover)
    1. Coffee brewing. 2. Coffee. I. Title.
TX817.C6W872   1995
641.8′77—dc20   95–15987
                                                CIP

8 7 6 5 4 3 2

This book is dedicated to all those wonderful people with whom I've shared a cup.

A big thanks to San Francisco Examiner Food Editor, Jim Woods, who, in 1987, suggested I write this book.

Without the help of Donna Jean Morris, Barney Taxel, Vicki Heil, Donald Lessne, Ted Lingle, Mike Carouso, and Tim Castle, this book would never have happened.

Mary Ward
November, 1992

TABLE OF CONTENTS

INTRODUCTION

This book is a celebration of the flavor of coffee. It joyously explores hundreds of possibilities for hot and cold coffee drinks, simple and complex, sweet and sophisticated. The author's expertise in blending flavors and aromas into delicious combinations inspires confident experimentation by the reader as well.

As beverages go, coffee is pretty new stuff. Coffee, in the form we know it, has been drunk for only a little under six centuries. Tea, by contrast, goes back a few thousand years, and wine may well be close to five-thousand years old. Once discovered though, coffee spread quickly, and today it is just beginning to challenge tea as the most popular beverage in several far-cast nations.

It makes sense then that people are still exploring the taste of coffee and how it gets along with other flavors. There may be rules about which wine to drink with which food but, so far, there are no rules about what to do with coffee. In fact, the tradition of flavoring coffee, or sweetening it, or mixing it with other beverages goes back to the first time coffee was drunk in the Middle East and Europe.

To this day, throughout much of the Middle East, coffee is served flavored with cardamom. In Vienna, coffee's first stop in Europe, shopkeepers served complex coffee drinks which included steamed milk, whipped cream, cinnamon, vanilla, and chocolate.

Probably the one thing most responsible for coffee's popularity is its gregarious nature: its boisterous flavor and aroma. There aren't a lot of flavors that coffee doesn't get along with. The recipe for Icy Java Mint, for example, is a surprising combination and a delicious drink.

Today, in the United States, coffee is undergoing a renaissance; Americans are rediscovering what a really good cup of coffee is and learning the importance of freshly roasted quality beans and proper storage and brewing. So intense is this resurgence that it has been predicted that by 1994, over one-third of the dollars spent on coffee in the U.S. will be on specialty coffee bought in the whole bean form. Of those sales, it has been predicted that over half will be flavored coffees, such as almond and chocolate raspberry.

Among coffee experts, there are purists who would argue that coffee should be drunk hot, black and unsweetened. Mary Ward, though, loves coffee too much to let it lead such a grim existence. Through her many years of experience in teaching consumers and retailers how to brew the best cup of coffee possible, she has learned that coffee can blend successfully with hundreds of flavors and surprising ingredients. A surprise to me was Cafe au Vin, a recipe which dares to blend a port wine with strong French Roast coffee. It reminded me that the original Arabic word for coffee was, in fact, the same word for wine: Qahwah. Cafe au Vin brings out the fruity complexity of the coffee, and the coffee adds a full-bodied yet silken texture to this amazing taste experience.

Mary Ward also understands that everyone is not a coffee connoisseur. Her style is down-to-earth, and she presents things in a clear, easy-to-read tone that belies her enthusiasm for the subject matter. So, while the recipes are new and even sometimes surprising, they are also easy-to-prepare, with readily obtainable ingredients.

Before getting into the recipes, however, Ms. Ward takes the reader through the basics of coffee. Her second chapter is indispensable to anyone who ever wondered what was wrong with their coffee or how they could make it taste better. Later on, she gives guidelines for creating blends in addition to sharing a few of her favorites. She even shows you how to roast your own coffee.

One feature completely unique to this coffee book is a nutritional analysis at the end of each recipe, which allows diet-conscious readers to choose drinks to suite their own particular regimen. Not only calories are counted, but carbohydrates, fat, percentage of calories from fat, cholesterol, sodium, potassium, caffeine, and calories from alcohol if alcohol is used.

Ms. Ward also points out that of all the ingredients listed above, one of the most suspect, caffeine, is in moderation, probably the least harmful.

This book can be an important first step for any reader who has yet to discover the pleasures of a truly extraordinary cup of coffee. It will show *you how to enjoy coffee much more and how to share it with your friends and family in new and scrumptious ways. But even if you've been reading everything written on coffee, I guarantee you'll find at least a few surprises, and some enjoyable ones at that.*

> *Timothy J. Castle*
> *President, Castle & Company*
> *Former President, Specialty Coffee*
> *Association of America*
> *Author: THE PERFECT CUP*
> *November, 1992*

1 ...AND THEN THERE WAS COFFEE

No wonder coffee is so important; it's the first thing you drink in the morning!

Coffee...America's breakfast beverage! And it's no wonder because coffee is not only a tasty refresher; it is also a safe but powerful stimulant. Yet, when you sip a cup of hot coffee, you're taking part in a tradition believed to be only a few centuries old: 1425 A.D.

Prior to this time, coffee cherries were eaten in various forms. A fermented drink, made from a sweetened tea of brewed leaves and fruit of the coffee tree, was popular as an intoxicant and stimulant. This was also drunk freshly brewed and unfermented.

As coffee houses became popular in Arabia in the mid-fifteenth century, the idea of these particular social gathering places moved into Europe. Viennese and Italian coffee houses were popular by the 16th century, and by the 17th century, coffee houses were being introduced into the new world, particularly into North America.

Coffee has since become America's favorite breakfast beverage as America drinks one-third of all coffee consumed. The peak years for coffee consumption were the early 1960s, when 75 percent of all adults drank at least one cup a day. Throughout the '70s and '80s, consumption leveled off, but we are now seeing growth in the area of gourmet coffees, specialty coffees, and decaffeinated coffees. Currently, 100 million people in the United States are coffee drinkers.

The taste of the '90s? Although Americans drink less coffee, they are drinking better coffee. The specialty and gourmet coffee industry is growing at the rate of 13 percent per year in this billion dollar industry. Specialty and gourmet coffees use the most select of coffee beans which have been grown in exotic parts of the world. They are roasted in small batches and sold through specialty and gourmet stores. Generally, specialty and gourmet coffees are 50 percent to 125 per cent more expensive than canned coffees and according to coffee aficionados, "worth every penny."

Good coffee starts with good coffee beans. Here's a brief description of the growth process:

FROM BUSH TO BEAN

The coffee tree looks a little like a camellia...with broad, dark, and shiny leaves. The leaves are camellia-shaped and two to five inches long, lining up in pairs on either side of the central stem. The jasmine-type flower is small, white, star shaped, and placed in clusters at the base of the leaves. The coffee tree or bush is generally planted from a seedling which has been cultivated from selected coffee cherries. In three years, the pruned and tended coffee tree will start to produce coffee cherries on a yearly cycle. A mature coffee tree can produce up to a pound and a half of coffee per year, depending on soil, climate, and general weather conditions.

There are hundreds of varieties of coffee trees, but 92 percent of these belong to either the arabica or robusta categories. Arabica beans are the select bean, lower in caffeine, flatter on the side, and generally more dense. Robusta beans are generally used for supermarket coffee blends, for internal consumption in countries where they are grown, and for instant coffee.

Coffee trees love the warm soil and balmy rainfall of countries located between the Tropic of Cancer and the Tropic of Capricorn. There, in the high altitudes, coffee thrives. Variations in soil, sunlight, and altitude produce changes in the coffee beans. Generally, the finest coffees are grown above three thousand feet, in rich soils, with an abundance of sunlight, and with soft, gentle rainfall.

The best coffee cherries are harvested when they are at maximum ripeness. At this point, they have taken on the appearance of a cherry. However, some arabica and all robusta beans are picked indiscriminately. This results in lack of uniformity in coffee product—some beans are overripe, some are underripe, and some perfectly ripe. Almost all coffee cherries are handpicked with a proficient coffee picker able to pick ten to twenty bushels of coffee cherries per day.

Once picked, the coffee cherries go to a local processing mill. Here, a process called pulping takes place. During this process, the coffee seed is washed, squeezed from the cherry, and sorted into sizes. In order to develop flavor, parchment coffee *(as it is now named) is fermented for up to thirty-six hours in a water tank. This being a critical part of the production process, fermentation is carefully attended by the mill owner. After fermentation, parchment coffee is hulled into the more familiar-looking coffee beans. These "washed" coffee beans are then sun dried. Although a lengthy sun dry period is preferred, many processing mills will speed the drying process by removing up to 8 percent of the moisture in mechanical dryers. Coffee processed in this way emphasizes the brightness of coffee flavors. When green coffee is ready for the market, it contains 12 percent moisture.*

In countries with little water and lots of sun, another type of processing takes place. Called natural process coffee, the coffee cherries are pulped then spread to dry in the sun. This process results in coffee with an earthier taste than the above method.

Once coffee has been processed and bagged, it is ready for distribution. Green coffee has a shelf life of only a few months. During this period, it constantly changes: maturing, mellowing, fading and staling depending on the time of year, the climate and the particular coffee.

A farmer sells coffee to an exporter, the exporter sells to an importer, and the importer sells to a roaster. Once coffee has been delivered to an importer and again after delivery to a roaster, the coffee is "cupped" (tasted). Three small samples of coffee are identically roasted and finely ground. Next, seven and one-half grams of each are placed into three, five and one-half ounce cups. Boiling water is added to the cup and the coffee allowed to steep for one minute. With the cuppers' nose just above the crust or surface of the coffee, the cups are stirred with a stainless steel soup spoon.

This is called "breaking the crust," and a "burst" of aroma is emitted. Then, each cup is carefully tested by the coffee dealer as a means of quality control through taste. In the trade, it is called "slurp and spit." This is quite an interesting sight to watch... and listen to. Incidentally, this process was developed in San Francisco by Folger's during the early 1900s.

Coffee, therefore, develops its unique flavor from a combination of type coffee plant grown, altitude, soil, amount of sun, and the method and quality of processing and milling.

THE ROASTING PROCESS

The traditional American roast is very light as this roast tends to emphasize acidity and fruitiness. In American roast the body is less developed. Dark roasts include French, Italian, and Espresso with darkness varying widely from coast to coast. Gourmet and specialty coffee shops will carry coffee by categories such as country of origin (e.g. Costa Rican, Hawaiian, Sumatran, Kenya), by darkness of roast (French Roast, Italian Roast, Light Roast), and by flavor (Amaretto, Irish Cream). Quality coffee shops take pride in their roasting.

The coffee roaster has the ultimate responsibility in producing great coffees for the customer. Coffee is placed in a coffee roasting drum and heated, while rotating, at over four hundred degrees. The master roaster will know exactly when the coffees have reached their peak flavors or their "roasting points." At this point, the coffee is quickly cooled and allowed to cure for two to three days before being sold.

Many Americans are interested in the roasting and flavoring of coffee beans. Gourmet and specialty coffee shops often carry green (or unroasted) coffees and recommend using a hot-air corn popper to roast coffee. If you roast coffee in this way, don't forget to cure it for two or three days before grinding and brewing. (I have included a recipe for oven-roasted coffee, see page 85).

Flavored coffees are roasted, then sprayed with artificial agents to give them different flavors. Currently, flavored coffees are almost 50 percent of specialty whole bean sales. These coffees, often Colombian in origin, are easy to make and several are listed on pages 86 to 89 of this book.

A coffee roaster may be a large operation which roasts several thousand pounds a day or it may be a specialty roaster who roasts only a few pounds a day. Because roasting is an art, master roasters oversee the process with care.

SELECTION

At the gourmet coffee shop or in many markets, you will see coffee labelled one of two ways:

1) BY THE COUNTRY OF GROWTH. (Sometimes part of the name will indicate the area in which the coffee is grown, such as "Costa Rica Tarrazu." Other times, the name might indicate where on the mountain range the coffee was grown, such as "Guatemalan Antigua" or "Sumatra Lintong.")

2) BY THE DARKNESS OF ROAST. (Italian and French refer to the darker roasts. Other names, such as city roast or European roast vary greatly from one region in the U.S. to another.)

Coffee is grown in Central and South America, the Caribbean, in Arab countries, in India, Africa, Hawaii, and in Indonesia and New Guinea. Characteristics of some of America's favorite specialty coffees are listed on page 12.

CHART 1

BRAZILIAN: medium-bodied, moderately acidic, pleasant earthiness

COLOMBIAN: full-bodied, richly flavored, slightly winey

COSTA RICAN TARRAZU: aromatic, heavy-bodied, hearty

ETHIOPIAN HARRAR: unusual, very aromatic, winey, wild grown

GUATEMALAN ANTIGUA: highly acidic, spicy, smokey flavor, very aromatic

INDIAN MYSORE: aromatic, light-bodied, slightly acidic, mellow, scarce

JAMAICA BLUE MOUNTAIN: aromatic, light body, mellow, mildly winey, very scarce

JAVA: full-bodied, rich, acidic, slightly smokey, spicy

KENYA AA: full-bodied, dry, winey aftertaste, acidic

KONA: medium-bodied, mildly winey, sweet, aromatic, nutty aftertaste

MEXICAN: aromatic, mild-bodied, mildly acidic

SUMATRAN: dry and heavy-bodied, low acidity, mellow, rich

TANZANIAN PEABERRY: sharp, winey acidity, medium-bodied, rich

YEMEN MOCHA: haunting chocolate aftertaste, winey acidity, sharp, grown wild

Sources: Timothy J. Castle, Michael P. Caruso

CAFFEINE

Coffee contains up to 2 percent caffeine. An average cup of coffee contains around 160 milligrams of caffeine. Caffeine enlarges blood vessels, in effect, stimulating the cerebral cortex. After drinking two or more cups of coffee, one might feel a "speed-up" of the thought processes, an increase in the association of ideas, a sense of euphoria, or an increased ability to learn and memorize numbers, concepts, and thought sequences.

Caffeine contributes to coffee's flavor. But, for some individuals, caffeine in coffee causes the "jitters." For this reason, we have included a chart (page 14) which notes the differences in caffeine levels. Most medical authorities find three hundred milligrams (mg) of caffeine to be a "safe" level. Note that just one cup of robusta coffee (the more inferior coffee) will provide that level of caffeine.

The quantity of caffeine in any given coffee will be reduced as that coffee is roasted to a darker version. A dark, waxy espresso, for example, will have less caffeine than a light Colombian.

CHART 2

How much caffeine in a 6 ounce cup of coffee?

COFFEE VARIETY	MILLIGRAMS
Ethiopian Mocha	160 mg
Santos	160 mg
Minas	163 mg
Peruvian	170 mg
Mexican	170 mg
Costa Rican	170 mg
Kive Arabican	177 mg
Nicaraguan	180 mg
Cameroon	180 mg
Guatemalan	187 mg
Salvador	187 mg
Java Arabican	187 mg
Venezuelan	192 mg
Colombian	195 mg
Cuban	195 mg
India Malabar	195 mg
Haitian	201 mg
Robusta Congo	327 mg
Robusta Uganda	327 mg

Source: Kenneth Anderson

Leading health organizations have studied the effects of caffeine on health. Their findings indicate that caffeinated coffee, when consumed in moderation, does not pose a threat to health. However, if you have a history of heart arrhythmias, stomach ulcers, fibrocystic disease, or if you are pregnant, you should be especially cautious of the amount you drink or ... drink decaffeinated coffee.

DECAFFEINATED COFFEE

Until the mid-'90s, decaffeinated coffee was considered to be flavorless, bitter and a poor substitute for regular coffee. As the process of decaffeination has improved, so has its market share with nearly 30 percent of the specialty and gourmet coffees being decaffeinated.

When coffee is decaffeinated, the solvent used may be either water or a chemical. These methods differ slightly but the process is the same: the beans are first softened by steaming. As they swell to twice their size, they are placed in a chemical solvent bath for decaffeination. Successful decaffeination depends on removing as much caffeine as possible while, at the same time, removing as little flavor as possible. It has never been demonstrated, however, that any of the chemically processed coffees expose consumers to any health risks whatsoever.

In Swiss Water process decaffeination, hot water, not chemicals, dissolves caffeine while leaving in as much of the flavor of coffee as possible.   The water is filtered through activated charcoal where caffeine is filtered out. More expensive than chemical removal of caffeine, this process is preferred by the many specialty coffee roasters.

In coffee taste tests, the average American may be able to detect a difference between Colombian Supremo, for example, and Guatemalan coffee. However, the same individuals often are hard-pressed to detect a difference between Colombian Supremo and Colombian Supremo DeCaf.

If you are concerned about your level of caffeine, you may want to try several other options: 50/50 blends (recipe on page 81); and Cafe au Lait (page 55), Cafe Latte (page 127), or Cafe con Leche (page 57). In these recipes, you'll have only one-half the caffeine of regular coffee. Also, evidence shows that your body will absorb only three hundred milligrams caffeine at any given time. Additional caffeine will provide no additional stimulation. So...after those two morning cups of coffee (or whenever you've had three hundred milligrams of caffeine), try a decaf blend or one of the great hot coffee recipes in this book made with decaffeinated coffee.

WHAT'S BREWING?

In the remainder of this book, I'll present a complete description on brewing and serving a perfect cup of coffee. Then, we'll go on to more than one hundred recipes. They are well-tested and should inspire your imagination and spark your creativity.

As a coffee lover, I guarantee if you read this book, you'll start to brew a great cup of coffee. You'll impress your friends and business associates with delicious recipes from this book, and you'll find that you'll make Every Cup of Coffee Count.

2

BREWING AND SERVING THE PERFECT CUP OF COFFEE

For me, the perfect cup of coffee comes from seven scoops of fine grind, dark-roasted blend of Mexican and Costa Rican coffee per ten, five-ounce cups of cold water and brewed at two hundred degrees for eight minutes. Pour this hot brew into my favorite white, warmed ceramic coffee mug, add a little hot milk, and that's the _perfect_ cup of coffee! When I brew this, my husband Joe has been known to comment, "The coffee tasted a little strong today." Joe likes a lightly roasted, 100 percent Colombian Coffee. Our daughter, Wendy, on the other hand, is a young wife, mother, and director of a day care center. She enjoys the economy of this week's whole bean specials. In other words, coffee taste and preference are personal: _my_ favorite coffee may not be your favorite even if brewed perfectly. Economy and value play a big part in decisions about coffee brewing.

When I conduct coffee taste tests on television or in malls, I'll find celebrities as well as consumers preferring the taste of a familiar coffee over that of a more exotic one. Recently, at The Gallery Mall in Philadelphia, up to 50 percent of the consumers preferred the taste of the $3.29 a pound supermarket coffee over that of the $32 a pound, properly brewed Blue Mountain Jamaican Coffee.

If you follow all six of the following rules, you'll have the perfect cup every time you brew coffee. And, it will be a coffee to your liking. The perfect cup of coffee includes these elements:

1) CLEANLINESS: Daily and monthly routine to keep the equipment sparkling clean.

2) COFFEE: A coffee roasted (and possibly blended) to your taste.

3) TASTE OF THE WATER: Choose cold tap or bottled spring water.

4) THE EQUIPMENT: Consider the various types of coffee makers.

5) STORAGE OF THE HOT BREW: Pour brewed coffee into a thermos to keep it hot and fresh.

6) PRESENTATION/SERVING THE COFFEE: From disposable cups to elegant glassware.

CLEANLINESS

The perfect cup of coffee starts with equipment which is scrupulously clean. From coffee filter to carafe to interior pipes, each part of your coffee maker needs to be kept clean on a regular basis.

Before you fill your coffee maker with water, clean it well. (I use a solution of baking soda and water because soap leaves a film and an aftertaste.) A clean coffee maker will brew great coffee because it will not impart the flavors of yesterday's coffee. So whether using a drip coffee maker, a percolator, an open-pot system, or an exotic Cona vacuum system, first scrub all interior glass, stainless, or aluminum equipment with baking soda and water.

Here's what I do: I keep a box of baking soda under my sink. In the morning, I simply wet a paper towel, scrub the interior of the carafe, then rinse it until the carafe shines. Once a week or so, I attack the exterior of the carafe with a stiff brush and the baking soda-water solution. This will clean out any residue of finely ground coffee from around the handle.

Don't forget to clean out the coffee filter with a good baking soda-water scrub. The filter picks up residues and stains from the coffee. When you remove these stains with baking soda and water, you'll let the fresh coffee brew through. Rinse the filter well to remove any tiny grinds of coffee that may be lodged inside. This will enable it to work more efficiently and speed up the brewing process.

Every thirty brewings (or once a month for most coffee maker owners), clean the interior of the coffee maker with a solution of one teaspoon white vinegar to a quart of water. You want to actually brew this mixture through the coffee maker. The vinegar will remove chemical deposits and buildup from the interior tubes of the coffee maker. This clean-up procedure will allow the water to pass through the coffee maker faster so that your equipment will work as efficiently as it did when it was new! Follow the vinegar rinse by brewing a cycle with clear, cold water.

In certain regions of the country, the chemical residues from water include iron, sulphur, lime, and other minerals. In those areas, ask your hardware store for a coffee maker cleaner-solvent.

When your coffee maker is spotlessly clean inside and outside, you'll be well on the way to brewing that perfect cup of coffee.

THE COFFEE

My twenty-six-year-old son, Jonathan, takes the art of brewing and drinking coffee seriously. A financial public relations man in New York City, Jon tells me that the criteria for judging good coffee is as follows: swish the hot coffee far back into your mouth...past the sweet and salty taste buds on the tip of your tongue to those finely tuned taste buds on the sides of your tongue. Now, swallow the coffee. Count to ten. If you can still savor the lively and bright flavor of the coffee you've consumed, you've had a memorable cup of coffee!

Selecting the right coffee bean for your palate is essential. A local gourmet shop I frequent has sixty-four different blends and roasts of coffee beans. That's a different coffee every morning for two months. But with that kind of selection, how do you start to choose the right one? In my coffee taste tests, I've found that most Americans are conditioned to drinking lightly roasted coffee. So, I'd recommend that you start off with the light city roast and work through the darker roasts and blends as you begin to savor the bright and heavier-bodied coffees.

To make sure the coffee is fresh, I'd recommend you buy it whole bean instead of ground. To tell whether it's been freshly roasted, look for a date on the package. Most packaged bean coffees are dated. Purchase the most recent roast, as bag bean coffees go stale quickly after roasting. Some of the new bag bean coffees, however, are vacuum packed and have a longer shelf life, but I still wouldn't purchase a bag of whole bean coffee if it looks as if the product turnover is low (if the bag is dusty, for example).

If you are buying your coffee from a bin in a gourmet store or supermarket, ask "When was this coffee roasted?" The sales person should be able to give you a roast date even if it was roasted off the premises. Insist on this information, or don't buy it. Also, look around and determine how the gourmet coffee looks. For example, is it uniform in color and size? Is it free from external matter such as stones and twigs? Also find out how the coffee is being stored. Is it in an airtight container to protect it from air and moisture?

As you proceed through your coffee drinking adventure, you may want to start ordering coffee from a specialty coffee company. These dependable companies are master roasters who send their coffees to you quickly after they are roasted so you know they are very fresh. For a discussion on thirty-six different American roasters, I recommend you read The Perfect Cup by Timothy J. Castle (Addison Wesley, 1991).

Another way to judge freshness of the roast is to ask for a "one bean sample" of the coffee. Now, bite the bean. If it has a crisp bite and a strong, mellow aftertaste, you'll know it is fresh. If it is rubbery and bitter, don't buy it! Or, you might want to purchase one-fourth pound of several coffees ... a 100 percent Colombian, a Kenya AA, and a House Blend. Then, perform your own coffee taste test.

After you've made a selection the next step is the grind. If you do not have a grinder, you'll need to grind your coffee at the store. Before grinding, allow the grinder to run for ten or fifteen seconds to rid itself of residues from the last batch of coffee. Next, grind your coffee to the finest grind possible without its going through holes in your coffee filter (fine grind if you are using paper filter liners). Then get it right home and into a well-sealed, air-tight, clean glass container. Store in a cool, dark place or in the coldest part of the freezer. For freshest flavor, I recommend grinding no more than one week's coffee at a time.

You may want to invest in a coffee grinder. There are two popular kinds: the blade coffee grinder and the burr coffee grinder. The least expensive coffee grinders are the blade types. The blades rotate much like a food processor or a blender. They are sharp and will pulverize your coffee beans to a coarse, medium, or fine grind. With a little experience, you'll know exactly the grind for your coffee maker. The advantage of the blade grinder is that you can add almonds, cinnamon sticks, roasted figs, and other additives to your coffee beans for new and different flavors. The disadvantage is the blade grinder does not grind coffee to the same consistency. In the same batch, some coffee may be very finely ground while some may be more coarsely ground. Many coffee purists insist that the blade grinder beats the coffee too much and this results in off-tasting coffee.

The burr grinder sends the coffee beans through two rotating wheels or burrs. This grinds your coffee to an even grind. Although more expensive, the burr type of grinder will grind coffee evenly and at several different grind settings. Some burr grinders have as many as eight settings from coarse to XX fine grind or espresso grind. Also, the capacity of these grinders is greater than for the blade grinder: you grind up to one cup of coffee at a time. The disadvantage is that burr grinders are designed to grind coffees, and you cannot use them for grinding almonds, cinnamon sticks, roasted figs, and those other additives.

There is some feeling among coffee purists that grinding coffee electrically will add heat to the grind and, thus, destroy some delicate coffee flavors.

So, many people still like to grind their coffee in an antique or other hand coffee grinder...or in a Turkish grinder. Although time consuming, coffee ground by hand is delicious!

In vacuum-canned coffees, the coffee is first ground, then packed in a can or bag. All air is removed. So, after grinding, the vacuum packing should prevent further deterioration of the ground coffee. However, vacuum-packed coffees often start with the more inferior blends that contain a high percentage of robusta beans. Whole bean gourmet coffees, on the other hand, are generally the higher quality arabica bean. In addition, because you are purchasing the coffee already ground, you'll have no way to ascertain the quality and uniformity of the coffee beans before grinding. In some vacuum-packed, ground coffees, the beans are burned, and malformed. Some even contain foreign objects such as sticks and twigs. All of these result in off-tasting coffees. When you purchase whole beans, you see what you are getting.

Still, having said all that, in my coffee taste tests, I oftentimes use a vacuum-packed ground coffee. *Sometimes it is the least expensive coffee on the grocer's shelf. Time after time, up to 50 percent of the consumers will prefer the taste of the vacuum-packed coffees. Since coffee selection is a matter of personal taste, if you enjoy vacuum-packed coffees and appreciate supermarket savings, purchase it that way. Just remember, after opening, seal the can well and store in a cool, dry place or in the freezer and brew it right for the finest flavor.*

THE WATER

O*kay. You've cleaned that coffee maker and purchased a really delightful coffee. What next? Well, since coffee is a blend of a little ground coffee and a lot of water, do you like the taste of your tap water? If you have off-tasting tap water, then you will have off-tasting coffee. You can remedy this by purchasing bottled spring water that is lively and oxygenated, ideally from a local spring. If you purchase bottled water, be sure NOT to purchase distilled water. It has no oxygen. Bottled spring water, on the other hand, will have bubbles rising to the surface, and this water will retain its oxygen even* *through refrigeration. One caution: distilled water comes in jugs similar to spring water jugs.*

M*y eighteen-month-old granddaughter, Melanie, was playing in the warm water at the kitchen sink the other day. She took a drink of the warm water and said, "Yuck." This was a reminder to me that cold water flavor is better than warm water flavor. Cold water has more oxygen in it and with that a more lively taste. So, if you like the taste of your tap water, let it run for a minute or two until it is as cold as it will get. Your coffee will have a better flavor. Also, the thermostat on most electric coffee makers is regulated to handle cold water, and the mechanics of the coffee maker work perfectly when the water is cold.*

S*hould you store your water in the refrigerator? I don't recommend storing tap water in the refrigerator. The reason is that when water is stored, you'll see little bubbles escaping to the top of the container. These bubbles are oxygen. Again, for maximum oxygen, just let your tap water run for a minute, then measure cold water into your brewing system.*

Now, let's say you've cleaned up the old coffee maker, you've purchased some great ground coffee, and you have brewed that coffee with cold, fresh water. Your coffee is still mediocre ... what's the problem?

THE EQUIPMENT

Possibly, that old electric equipment is not heating the water hot enough. Perhaps, the thermostat is not working properly. Maybe it's just worn out!

DRIP COFFEE MAKERS

At present, many Americans who drink coffee brew it in a drip coffee maker. In a drip coffee maker, ground coffee is placed in the upper filter and hot water is poured over it. The brewed coffee trickles through the filter and into the lower compartment or carafe. The electric drip coffee maker will heat the water, brew the coffee, then cut back the temperature for storage. The proper brew temperature for coffee is right around two hundred degrees. At two hundred degrees, the right coffee flavors are extracted. A temperature lower than 180 or 190 degrees, results in a "muddy" taste to the coffee, and temperatures higher than two hundred degrees result in a bitter flavor to the coffee.

If you use an electric drip coffee maker, you can measure the temperature of the brewing water. Here's how: take a clean oven thermometer and immerse it into your coffee carafe. When the coffee is brewed into the carafe, make sure the stream of water pours over the oven thermometer. After six to seven minutes, the coffee temperature will be at its peak, so look at the thermometer. You'll have a fairly accurate reading of the heat of your brew water.

If you use an inexpensive, non-electric glass drip coffee maker, water temperature is very important. Make sure the water poured over those grounds is just below boiling.

As important as the temperature of the coffee is the amount of time the hot water will be in *contact with the coffee grounds. Many electric coffee makers, both drip and percolator, are known to take twelve to fifteen or even twenty minutes to brew coffee. By coffee purist standards, that's just too long for the water to be in contact with coffee grounds. Coffee should be in contact with the very hot water for no longer than eight to ten minutes. After that, bitter flavors develop.*

Much has been written about the coffee makers with cone filter. In this type filter, hot water sprays over the grounds and is forced through one or more openings at the bottom of the cone...sort of a gravity pull system. Therefore, the grounds are penetrated more evenly by the hot water than a filter with a flat bottom. Most drip coffee filters utilize filter papers and require fine grind coffee. Although finely ground coffee offers better yield per pound of coffee, coffee purists would argue that paper filters absorb some of coffees' rich flavor. One of my coffee makers has a fine mesh filter, and though the clean-up is more difficult, this filter does make very good coffee.

Incidentally, if you are looking for the origin of a particular coffee maker, just check the product packaging. It will say, in large print, where the product was manufactured. It will also tell whether the product was approved by Underwriter's Laboratories (UL). UL specifies product guidelines for coffee makers. These specifications include a burn-proof exterior as well as interior electrical specifications. Do not purchase a coffee maker that is not UL approved.

New models of the electric drip coffee makers include a variety of features. Some have conveniences such as a drip stop which allows you to pour a cup of coffee during the brew cycle. Most manufacturers feature a one or two cup coffee maker which brews one or two cups of coffee in under five minutes. Several manufacturers feature coffee makers that store the coffee in a thermos. When purchasing a coffee maker, the first question to your sales person should be, "Which of these coffee makers has the hottest brew cycle ... up to two hundred degrees?" and "How long does it take to brew a pot of coffee?" Sales personnel have been trained with this information. Let them guide you and explain convenience features.

If you are purchasing a new coffee maker, I'd strongly suggest that you check it for comfort. The scientific name for the engineering study of comfort is "ergonomics." Check out the ergonomics of the unit. You'll want to practice lifting the carafe to test the feel of the handle. Is it a sturdy carafe handle? Is the handle attached well to the appliance? Will it pour? Remember, in a year's time, a carafe may be lifted as many as 8 times a day or 56 times a week, or 2,912 times a year! You want to make sure that it is easy and comfortable to lift.

THE PERCOLATOR

Percolators, invented in 1829, bring to mind images of coffee perking over the campfire or on the electric range. Who can forget the classic Maxwell House Coffee commercial with the jingle..."good to the last drop."

In a drip coffee maker, hot water is sprayed over the grounds. A percolator utilizes a pressurized brewing environment which acts like a piston in constantly circulating the water.

In the preparation for perking top-of-the-stove coffee, the water oftentimes boiled, burning the coffee and resulting in a bitter brew. The first electric percolators, in the 1930s , were not much of an improvement as the brew temperature was too hot or too cool and lasted much too long (as long as 20 minutes).

Today's electric percolators are a vast improvement over the outdated models, perking at a temperature of 193 degrees with a brew time as short as four minutes. Properly perked coffee has a robust, well-developed flavor which is preferred by many Americans. Other advantages: percolators do not require paper filters.

OPEN-POT BREWING

If you like a coffee which is richer and heavier, a top-of-the-stove, open-pot coffee maker may be for you. In open-pot brewing, coffee grounds are steeped in a pot of hot water, strained and served (see recipes pages 61 and 71).

One popular type of open-pot brewing is the French Press, or plunger pot. The system utilizes a pot which is a narrow glass cylinder. Coffee and near-boiling water are put into this cylinder. Then, a tight-fitting, meshed screen plunger is inserted. After the coffee has steeped for three minutes, the plunger is pushed through the coffee, clarifying it and forcing the grinds to the bottom. Coffee is served directly from the cylinder. Although expensive, the French Press makes a rich, heavy-bodied cup of coffee. The advantages are clear: it is portable and easy. Full-bodied coffee may be prepared table side. (See picture page 20).

There are many more kinds of coffee brewing systems available from the functional Neapolitan flip drip to elegant Cona vacuum systems to the table-side Italian servers. It's a good idea to shop at department stores, gourmet shops, specialty coffee stores as well as mass merchants to find the coffee system that's best for your lifestyle.

STORAGE OF COFFEE

So, you've brewed that perfect cup of coffee. It is hot, fresh tasting, and memorable. How can you preserve that delicious coffee flavor?

Coffee is very temperature sensitive. Once brewed, it starts to rapidly deteriorate. Most electric coffee makers hold coffee at 160 to 170 degrees. However, even at this temperature, coffee will start to taste noticeably bitter in twenty minutes. In an hour, the coffee is very bitter. What to do?

First, brew only what will be consumed in an hour. If that's half a pot, then brew half a pot. You may want to invest in a quality thermos or in a coffee making system that brews into a thermos. One caution in using the thermos: make sure the thermos is glass lined. Plastic or other composition material thermos will impart off flavors. And with a glass-lined thermos, you are able to thoroughly clean the thermos with a solution of baking soda and water.

The design of the thermos is also important. The tall, slender thermos is designed to hold
and seal in the heat from coffee, keeping it hot and
fresh tasting for six to eight hours. The "roly poly"
thermos shape exposes more coffee surface to air;
coffee will cool more quickly in such a thermos.

But let's say you have coffee in your glass
carafe, it was brewed one hour ago, and you've
turned off the heat. Should you reheat the coffee in
the microwave? Again, that's a personal taste.
Cooled, reheated coffee doesn't taste very good.
However, it does have all the caffeine; and if you're
after that quick bit of caffeine, reheated coffee will
give you that. Because coffee brewing is important to
me, I want to make "every cup of coffee count."
Rather than reheat old coffee, I use a two-cup coffee
maker...one cup in two minutes, forty seconds...faster
than my microwave would heat a cup of water.

PRESENTATION/SERVING

Have you ever been invited to have a cup
of coffee, then given a cup that looks like it was used

for 250 years because it is so stained and dirty? Do you like the taste of your coffee in Styrofoam or paper cups? How about the plastic cups for the top of the car dashboard? The serving and presentation of coffee is every bit as important as the other elements in brewing.

First, coffee cups must be very clean. The coffee purist will wash coffee cups by hand, scrubbing out the coffee ring with baking soda and water. Allow cups to drain to sparkling dry. If you serve guests from a ceramic or silver coffee set, make sure the interiors are scrubbed well with baking soda and water. I've found that the dishwasher doesn't always clean coffee stains from coffee cups. For that perfect cup of coffee, scrub the cups with baking soda and water and rinse thoroughly.

For people who add accoutrements to their coffee, the perfect creamer is warmed whole milk or half and half. If you use powdered creamer, you'll have off-tasting coffee. For sweetening, I'd suggest simple syrup: a boiled mixture of 50 percent sugar, 50 percent water (recipe on page 102). For those who want a more continental flavor, stir with a cinnamon stick.

If you must drink your coffee in Styrofoam cups, make sure you rinse them first with hot water to remove any particles that could cause off-tasting coffee. If you have a decision between waxed cardboard coffee cups or Styrofoam coffee cups, the Styrofoam will deliver more true coffee flavor. Oftentimes, the wax from the cardboard cup will melt into the coffee.

My favorite material for coffee cups is earthenware. Earthenware washes well and really holds the heat. A good coffee cup should keep coffee hot for fifteen minutes. Glass, ceramic, and plastic coffee cups and mugs do not hold heat very long. Dainty china demitasse cups and delicate bone china tea cups make lovely receptacles for coffee, but the coffee will simply not stay hot very long.

If you are using glass or other delicate materials, one good idea is to heat the cup before you pour the coffee. Simply pour hot water in the cup and allow to stand for five minutes. This will help the glass or china cup to retain the heat of the hot coffee.

Another elegant presentation is the wine or Irish whiskey glass. I like to use wide-lipped wine glasses for after dinner coffees. They are easy to drink from and make a nice presentation. If you plan to do this, pretest the wine glass to make sure it will handle the heat of the hot coffee.

When you are buying demitasse cups, coffee cups, coffee mugs, or delicate tea cups, it's a good idea to test them before purchase. Some of the most beautiful sets are nearly impossible to drink from and to handle. If you test them, you'll know which ones work.

So, serve yourselves and your guests perfectly brewed coffee from sparkling clean, hot coffee mugs and you'll serve the best coffee in the area. Guaranteed!

A few years ago, my reputation was on the line. I was going through the brew steps for WABC's Live! with Regis Philbin and Kathie Lee

Gifford. We were having a coffee taste test: Mary's coffee vs. Sy's coffee. Now, Sy was the WABC propman, and I had tasted his coffee. It was a hot, heavy-bodied cup made in a large percolator-style coffee maker. I was using a European-styled coffee maker with A & P's One Hundred Percent Colombian Whole Bean Coffee (inexpensive at $3.98 per pound). Sy, incidentally, used Maxwell House Vacuum Coffee at $7.98 for a two-pound can. The coffee taste tester was a coffee lover from Queens. Her name was Barbara, and she looked like a real coffee drinker. I had brewed a perfect cup of coffee, so when Regis said, "Is the best coffee number one or number two?" I was only a bit apprehensive. Barbara se-lected number one, my coffee. Barbara felt Sy's coffee had a "burned" taste. Sy's coffee, incidentally, was brewed at six in the morning for this nine o'clock morning show. Mine was brewed at eight-thirty. All personal preferences aside, I won that taste test because my coffee was fresher.

THE BREW CYCLE

For the brew cycle, measure good-tasting, cold, fresh water into your scrupulously clean coffee maker. Consider how much coffee you plan to drink *in the next hour. Now, measure one tablespoon (or less) freshly ground coffee per five ounce cup of water. Turn on the coffee maker. The coffee should take no longer than one minute per cup to brew...for an eight cup pot, that's eight minutes. When the coffee is finished brewing, store on heat for one hour or pour into a thermos. When serving, pour into clean, hot earthenware or ceramic mugs. Serve with half and half or whole milk and simple syrup.*

As to the correct amount of coffee, manufacturers generally recommend one scoop (just under one tablespoon) per five or six ounce cup of water. For many Americans, that's just too strong. In coffee taste tests, I find that seven scoops for a ten-cup coffee maker, or eight scoops for a twelve-cup coffee maker suits nearly every taste. Incidentally, for my own taste, I use one scoop per five ounce cup of water. If you are measuring the fresh beans into a grinder, use a rounded scoop to compensate for settling out of the ground coffee.

Get brewing but remember, every time you brew coffee, you will be performing your own coffee taste test. Make every Cup of Coffee Count!

3 HOT COFFEES

How many ways can you serve hot coffee? An infinite number, but here we have a collection of over forty-five favorite hot coffees. Any of these recipes may be made with your favorite ground coffees. Whether the coffee is decaffeinated, caffeinated, or flavored, all recipes will "work!"

From basic Scandinavian Egg Coffee and the rich tasting Mochas, to the aristocratic Italian favorites, you're going to find ways to brew hot coffees for your next Kaffee Klatch, for your next dinner party, and for those moments of relaxation with "a cup!"

As we start with this section, you will notice that almost all of the recipes contain a nutrient analysis. Many individuals today like to know nutrients in their foods so that they may tabulate their daily totals. The data for this nutrient analysis comes from NUTRITIONIST III, a software program from N-SQUARED COMPUTING in Silverton, Oregon.

Recipes have been analyzed for amounts of calories, grams of carbohydrate, grams of protein, grams of fat, percentage of calories from fat, cholesterol, sodium, potassium, caffeine, and percentage of calories from alcohol (in recipes containing alcohol). Sources of information along with NUTRITIONIST III include the National Academy of Science's 1980 Recommended Daily Dietary Allowances (RDA), Bowles and Church's 14th Edition, United States Department of Agriculture's Bulletin #72, and individual manufacturer's data.

How to use this information? Always look at the number of calories...then the percentage of calories from fat. The USDA recommends a total diet containing no more than 30 percent calories from fat. In addition, you may want to count milligrams of cholesterol, sodium and potassium. Your doctor can give you his recommendations for your level of fats and cholesterol. RDA for sodium is 2200 mg and for potassium, 3750. The level of caffeine generally regarded as safe is 300 milligrams. Of course, decaffeinated coffee may be substituted for regular coffee in any recipe.

To reduce the calorie and fat levels in any recipe, reduce the amount of sugar and cream. Substitute skimmed milk for whole milk, and evaporated, skimmed milk may be substituted for cream. Frozen yogurt or ice milk may be substituted for ice cream in any recipe. In recipes containing alcohol, you will reduce calories and alcohol by heating the alcohol to a boiling point. After the alcohol has boiled away, the flavor remains with far fewer calories.

All recipes in this book have been triple tested, and are easy to read, and use. Also, almost all of the ingredients are readily available at your supermarket.

BLACK FOREST COFFEE

8 ounces freshly brewed, French roast coffee (regular or decaffeinated)

4 tablespoons chocolate syrup

2 tablespoons maraschino cherry juice

1/4 cup sweetened whipped cream

1 tablespoon shaved chocolate or chocolate chips

2 maraschino cherries

This is a coffee to serve instead of dessert. It is simple to prepare, and the ingredients make you think of Black Forest Cake! Use your finest china cups or Irish coffee glasses for an elegant presentation.

Serves: 2

Combine coffee, chocolate syrup, and cherry juice. Divide into two warm china cups or Irish coffee glasses, six ounces each. Top with whipped cream, shaved chocolate, and a maraschino cherry.

Each serving: 233 calories; 18 gm carbohydrates; 2 gm protein; 19 gm fat (68% calories from fat); 33 mg cholesterol; 15 mg sodium; 109 mg potassium; 86 mg caffeine (made with regular coffee).

CAFE AU LAIT

Our twenty-fifth wedding anniversary was spent in Chamonix, France, with our three college-aged children. In the morning, before skiing, we started the day with gulps of cafe au lait, croissant, and baguettes. What a joy!

Serves: 4

2 cups
hot French
roast coffee
(regular or
decaffeinated)

2 cups hot
milk, 2%
milk fat

Place hot coffee in a hot coffee pot. In the second hot coffee pot, place the milk. Pour simultaneously from both pots into warm eight ounce cups.

Each serving: 38 calories; 4 gm carbohydrate; 2 gm protein; 1 gm fat (31% of calories from fat); 5 mg cholesterol; 39 mg sodium; 230 mg potassium; 139 mg caffeine (made with regular coffee).

CAFE BORGIA

2 cups hot
chocolate

2 cups strong,
hot Italian roast
coffee (regular or
decaffeinated)

1/2 cup
sweetened
whipped cream

grated orange
peel for garnish

Here's an authentic Italian recipe. It uses the traditional, strong Italian Roast coffee and combines it with the sweetness of orange. Try this on a leisurely afternoon...perhaps before your next bocce game.

Serves: 4

Combine hot chocolate with coffee. Pour into four, eight ounce, warm coffee mugs. Top with whipped cream and sprinkle with grated orange peel.

Each serving: 153 calories; 14 gm carbohydrates; 5 gm protein; 7 gm fat (51% calories from fat); 30 mg cholesterol; 88 mg sodium; 300 mg potassium; 72 mg caffeine (made with regular coffee).

Cafe con Leche

When Americans travel, they oftentimes find the coffee roast darker than they prefer. Adding hot milk will give this strong coffee a more familiar flavor. In all Spanish-speaking countries, and many other countries, by simply saying ,"con leche," hot milk will be served. The Mexican version of Cafe Con Leche follows.

Serves: 4

Combine coffee with hot milk and sugar. Divide evenly between four warm mugs. Place a cinnamon stick in each.

Each serving: 76 calories; 9 gm carbohydrate; 4 gm protein; 2 gm fat (24% calories from fat); 9 mg cholesterol; 65 mg sodium; 256 mg potassium; 70 mg caffeine (made with regular coffee).

**2 cups
strong coffee
(preferably
Mexican)**

**2 cups
hot milk,
2% milk fat**

**1 tablespoon
granulated
sugar**

**4 small sticks
cinnamon**

CAFE DE OLLA

2 cups water

1/4 cup Mexican coffee, coarsely ground

1 large stick cinnamon

1 tablespoon brown sugar

Mexican coffee, as in many Latin American countries, is boiled and strained through cloth or some other material. In Mexico, however, cinnamon and brown sugar are the accepted additives. They add sweetness and spice. This richly flavored coffee is perfect for a mid-morning coffee break.

Serves: 2

Place water, coffee, cinnamon, and brown sugar in a saucepan and bring to a boil. Reduce heat and simmer another three to five minutes. Strain through a fine strainer. Serve in large, warm, heavy mugs.

Each serving: 42 calories; 8 gm carbohydrate; 0 protein; 0 fat; 0 cholesterol; 18 mg sodium; 295 mg potassium; 278 mg caffeine (made with regular coffee).

CARIBBEAN COFFEE

Here's a rich, dark coffee blend with a tropical taste. This recipe was a hit at a recent Caribbean Cooking School I taught in south Florida. I like to serve it with fruit ice for a light dessert.

Serves: 8

With hammer and nail, drive two holes into the coconut. Drain coconut liquid into saucepan. Bake whole coconut at 300° F. for thirty minutes to release coconut meat from hard shell. Grate fresh coconut (about one cup).

Place saucepan over low heat and combine grated coconut, coconut liquid, and milk. Heat until creamy. Strain, reserving both grated coconut and hot milk mixture. Toast grated coconut under broiler or in fry pan on top of range.

In warmed mugs, blend hot coconut milk with equal amounts of hot coffee. Sweeten with sugar. Sprinkle with toasted coconut.

1 medium
coconut

2 cups milk,
2% milk fat

4 cups dark,
rich coffee
(Costa Rican,
if possible)

1 tablespoon
sugar

Each serving: 27 calories; 8 gm carbohydrate; 3 gm protein; 10 gm fat; 67% calories from fat); 5 mg cholesterol; 40 mg sodium; 255 mg potassium; 70 mg caffeine (made with regular coffee).

CAFE MEXICANO

4 teaspoons
chocolate syrup

1/2 cup
whipping cream

3/4 teaspoon
cinnamon,
divided into
2 parts

1/4 teaspoon
nutmeg

1 tablespoon
sugar

1-1/2 cups
hot, strong coffee
(preferably
Mexican)

Here's my favorite Mocha. It's a spicy and rich mocha...a great pick-me-up for a cold, rainy afternoon.

Serves: 4

Put one teaspoon chocolate syrup into each of four, four ounce, warm cups. Combine whipping cream, one-fourth teaspoon cinnamon, nutmeg, and sugar. Whip into soft peaks. Stir remaining one-half teaspoon cinnamon into hot coffee. Pour coffee into cups. Stir to blend with syrup. Top with spiced whipped cream.

Each serving: 130 calories; 8 gm carbohydrates; 1 gm protein; 11 m fat (74% calories from fat); 41 mg cholesterol; 17 mg sodium; 91 mg potassium; 53 mg caffeine (made with regular coffee).

COSTA RICA CAFEZINHO

Traditionally, the Costa Rican coffee processed for internal consumption may have up to 12 percent sugar roasted with the coffee beans. In the United States, Costa Rican coffee is roasted without the sweetener, and the flavor is delicate and bright. Incidentally, the coffee strainer, or Cafezinho, is sometimes referred to as the "sock." Serve Costa Rican coffee with light, crispy cookies as an afternoon snack!

Serves: 4

> 2 cups
> cold water
>
> 8 tablespoons
> finely ground
> Costa Rican
> coffee
> (preferably
> from the
> Tarrazu region)
>
> 1 teaspoon
> sugar

Measure water into a saucepan and bring to a boil. Meanwhile, place the coffee into a strainer lined with several layers of cheesecloth or into a cafezinho bag. Pour the boiled water into the bag, holding over a receptacle until all water has seeped through. Add sugar and serve in warm, four-ounce demitasse cups.

Each serving: 24 calories; 4 gm carbohydrates; 0 gm protein; 0 gm fat; 0 mg cholesterol; 16 mg sodium; 256 mg potassium; 278 mg caffeine (made with regular coffee).

TURKISH COFFEE

If you don't have the traditional, long-handled Ibrik, use any saucepan. This makes a fine, afternoon coffee.

Serves: 4

In Ibrik or saucepan, heat water to luke-warm. Add coffee and sugar. Stir. Bring to a boil over medium heat. Pour off half of coffee into warm demitassee cups. Boil remaining coffee again. Remove from heat and spoon some of the creamy foam of coffee into each cup. Fill cups, but do not stir coffee once it has been poured. In Arabic, the foam is called "the face of the coffee"--and you lose face if you serve coffee without it!

1-1/2 cups cold water

4 teaspoons French or Italian roast coffee (regular or decaffeinated), ground to finest grind possible

4 teaspoons granulated sugar

Each serving: 23 calories; 5 gm carbohydrates; 0 gm protein; 0 gm fat ; 0 mg cholesterol; 8 mg sodium; 136 mg potassium; 139 mg caffeine (made with regular coffee).

CAFE EUROPA

1 egg white

1/4 teaspoon
vanilla extract

1 cup
strong, hot
coffee
(preferably
dark roast)

2 tablespoons
half and half

*In this unique coffee, the egg white will
float to the top of the cup with swirls of
brown circulated through it.*

Serves: 2

Beat egg white with vanilla until stiff.
Divide between two, warmed coffee
mugs. Top with coffee and half and half.

Each serving: 32calories; 1 gm carbohydrates; 2 gm
protein; 2 gm fat (54% calories from fat); 6 mg cholesterol; 35 mg sodium; 106 mg potassium; 70 mg caffeine
(made with regular coffee).

MEDITERRANEAN COFFEE

In this recipe, the spices enhance the deep flavor of the Italian roast. This is a great coffee to serve after a light meal. Serve it HOT!

Serves: 8

Combine first six ingredients in a saucepan. Bring to just under the boiling point over medium-high heat. Reduce heat and simmer until ready to serve. Strain into warmed coffee mugs and top with the whipped cream and orange and lemon twists.

Each serving: 109 calories; 12 mg carbohydrates; 1 protein; 7 gm fat (53% calories from fat); 17 mg cholesterol; 13 mg sodium; 160 mg potassium; 142 mg caffeine (made with regular coffee).

8 cups
freshly brewed,
strong coffee
(preferably
Italian roast
coffee)

1/3 cup
granulated sugar

1/4 cup
chocolate syrup

4 cinnamon
sticks

1-1/2 teaspoons
whole cloves

1/2 teaspoon
aniseed, tied in
a cheesecloth

1/2 cup
sweetened,
whipped cream
for garnish

orange and
lemon twists

SPICY AUSTRIAN COFFEE

Serves: 4

**4 strips,
3 inch by
1/2 inch,
orange peel**

**4 strips,
1 inch by
1/2 inch,
lemon peel**

20 whole cloves

**4 tablespoons
ground coffee,
(preferably
Sumatran)**

**1 quart
cold water**

**2 teaspoons
(or less) brown
sugar**

Place orange peel, lemon peel, and cloves into the bottom of a drip coffee carafe. Brew coffee as directed so that hot coffee drips onto spices. Divide between four, warmed mugs. Sweeten to taste.

Each serving: 22 calories; 4 gm carbohydrates; 0 gm protein; 0 gm fat ; 0 mg cholesterol; 12 mg sodium; 181 mg potassium; 186 mg caffeine (made with regular coffee).

Mocha Mugs

Ever get so cold you thought you'd never warm up? Well, here's an answer for heating up cold toes and noses. Make it up in advance and have it ready for apres ski...or after a cold, windy golf round!

Serves: 4

Stir cocoa and sugar together in a saucepan. Stir in hot coffee and cold milk. Heat, stirring frequently, until it is simmering. Remove from heat and stir in vanilla.

Ladle chocolate mixture into four, eight-ounce mugs (or into a thirty-two ounce thermos). Top each serving with whipped cream, then ground cinnamon.

Each serving: 311 calories; 34 gm carbohydrate; 6 gm protein; 19 gm fat (52% calories from fat); 77 mg sodium; 367 mg potassium; 82 mg caffeine (made with regular coffee).

1/3 cup unsweetened cocoa powder

1/2 cup sugar

2 cups hot, freshly brewed coffee (regular or decaffeinated)

2 cups milk, 2% milk fat

1/2 teaspoon pure vanilla extract

1/2 cup whipping cream, whipped

ground cinnamon

NUTTY COFFEE NOG

1 tablespoon
brown sugar

1 egg yolk

1/2 cup cream

1 cup freshly
brewed, hot
coffee
(regular or
decaffeinated)

nutmeg

*Here's a very different kind of
coffee...actually creamy and rich with just
a hint of traditional nog flavor. It's a great
recipe to serve with holiday brunch.*

Serves: 2

Combine sugar and egg yolk; beat well.
In a small saucepan, heat cream. Slowly
whisk in egg/sugar mixture and carefully
heat to just below boiling. Remove from
heat. Divide coffee among two warmed
cups and top with cream/egg mixture.
Sprinkle with nutmeg.

Each serving: 139 calories; 10 gm carbohydrate; 3 gm
protein; 10 gm fat (63% calories from fat); 158 mg
cholesterol; 35 mg sodium; 177 mg potassium; 70 mg
caffeine (made with regular coffee).

COFFEE GROG

A special treat for a cold winter's day...delightfully hot and sweet. Make the grog mix in advance; it will stay fresh for several weeks.

Serves: 6

To make Grog mix, cream all ingredients until well blended.

To make Coffee Grog, divide grog mix between six, warm mugs. Divide remaining ingredients between mugs. Stir well.

Each serving: 233 calories; 36 gm carbohydrates; trace protein; 10 gm fat (38% calories from fat); 33 mg cholesterol; 61 mg sodium; 211 mg potassium; 70 mg caffeine (made with regular coffee).

Grog mix:
2 tablespoons softened butter

1 cup brown sugar

1/4 teaspoon ground cloves

1/4 teaspoon freshly ground nutmeg

1/4 teaspoon cinnamon

Coffee Grog:
6 strips, 3 inch by 1/2 inch, orange peel

6 strips, 1 inch by 1/2 inch, lemon peel

1/2 cup heavy cream, warmed

3 cups hot coffee, preferably dark roast

ORANGE COFFEE

1 orange slice

4 ounces strong, hot coffee (regular or decaffeinated)

4 ounces hot chocolate

1/4 cup sweetened whipped cream

1/8 teaspoon cinnamon

I once served this coffee to food editors. It was easy to take the ingredients with me to the newsroom...and the flavors were appreciated by all!

Serves: 1

Place an orange slice into a warm, eight-ounce mug. Pour coffee and hot chocolate over it. Top with sweetened whipped cream and sprinkle with cinnamon.

Each serving: 100 calories; 14 gm carbohydrate; 3 gm protein; 4 gm fat (33% calories from fat); 13 mg cholesterol; 96 mg sodium; 233 mg potassium; 72 gm caffeine (made with regular coffee).

SCANDINAVIAN EGG COFFEE

Scandinavians take special pride in making coffee this old-fashioned way. It is also a very convenient idea for campers. The clarifying effect of the egg white helps the coffee to sparkle!

Serves: 8

4-1/2 quarts water

1-1/2 cups regular grind, Scandinavian or Danish blend coffee

1 egg white

1/2 cup cold water

In a large saucepan (or campfire coffee pot), bring the four and one-half quarts water to a boil. Combine coffee and egg white, reserving the shell. Stir the coffee-egg mixture and shell into the boiling water. Return to a boil. Remove from heat and allow to steep for two minutes. Slowly pour in cold water to help settle the grounds. Strain, and serve into large, warm mugs.

Each serving: 10 calories; 1 gm carbohydrates; trace protein; 0 fat; 0 mg cholesterol; 14 mg sodium; 134 mg potassium; 139 mg caffeine (made with regular coffee).

SOUTH OF THE BORDER COFFEE COOLER

2 cups hot chocolate

2 cups freshly brewed coffee (preferably Mexican)

1 tablespoon cinnamon

1/2 pint whipping cream

1/4 teaspoon cinnamon

1/4 teaspoon nutmeg

1 tablespoon sugar

1 tablespoon grated chocolate for garnish

Although this is a hot beverage, the combination of spices is certain to cool you off on a hot day. I love to serve this with cinnamon toast.

Serves: 4

Combine hot chocolate, coffee, and cinnamon in a coffee carafe over a warmer. Whip cream with cinnamon, nutmeg, and sugar. Divide coffee mixture into four mugs. Top with whipped cream and grated chocolate.

Each serving: 283 calories; 17 gm carbohydrate; 3 gm protein; 23 gm fat (72% calories from fat); 83 mg cholesterol; 100 mg sodium; 234 mg potassium; 73 mg caffeine (made with regular coffee).

SPICED MOCHA MUGS

Mocha is a popular beverage apres ski...as well as on the slopes. In fact, slope-side restaurants in elegant ski resorts such as Sun Valley, Idaho, feature mocha as a hot beverage. Here's a 1990's version of this old favorite!

Serves: 4

Pour water into a saucepan. Add cinnamon, cloves, and allspice and bring to a boil. Simmer for ten minutes. Cool, then strain. Place water into coffee maker with ground coffee and brew according to manufacturers instructions. Whip cold whipping cream with cocoa, sugar, and vanilla. Pour hot coffee into large, warm coffee mugs, and top with generous dollops of chocolate whipped cream.

Each serving: 309 calories; 19 gm carbohydrate; 3 gm protein; 26 gm fat (73% calories from fat); 66 mg cholesterol; 37 mg sodium; 433 mg potassium; 292 mg caffeine (made with regular coffee).

4 cups
cold water

2 sticks
cinnamon,
1 inch each

12 whole cloves

8 allspice
berries

4 ounces
ground coffee
(regular or
decaffeinated)

1 cup
whipping cream

1/4 cup
unsweetened
cocoa

1/4 cup
granulated
sugar

1 teaspoon
pure vanilla
extract

SPICED VIENNESE COFFEE

4 cinnamon sticks

8 cloves

8 allspice berries

5 cups cold water

8 tablespoons finely ground gourmet coffee (regular or decaffeinated)

1/2 cup sweetened whipped cream

cinnamon

Dan Cox, owner of Green Mountain Coffee Roasters in Waterbury, Vermont, says this is a favorite way to keep warm through the cold, Vermont winters.

Serves: 8

Place cinnamon sticks, cloves, and allspice berries into an eight or ten cup coffee carafe. Measure cold water into the coffee maker. Using ground coffee, brew according to manufacturer's instructions. Allow the coffee to steep for fifteen minutes after brewing. Strain into eight, eight ounce, warmed coffee mugs (or into a thermos). Garnish with whipped cream and a sprinkle of ground cinnamon.

Each serving: 17 calories; 1 gm carbohydrate; 0 protein; 1 gm fat (59% calories from fat); 3 mg cholesterol; 12 mg sodium; 124 mg potassium; 121 mg caffeine (made with regular coffee).

T OFFEE COFFEE

I recently took this beverage with me in a thermos for a spot on WIBC Radio in Indianapolis. Jeff Pidgeon, the morning disc jockey, appreciated the rich blending of flavors.

Serves: 4

Sift sugar into a medium-sized, moderately hot, heavy skillet, stirring constantly until all the sugar is melted and is a rich caramel color. Remove from heat and carefully add hot water, stirring until all caramel is dissolved and is maple-syrup consistency. Add hot chocolate and coffee and simmer to blend. Serve in heavy coffee mugs.

1/4 cup
granulated
sugar

3/4 cup
hot water

1-1/2 cups
hot chocolate

2 cups freshly
brewed, strong
coffee
(regular or
decaffeinated)

Each serving: 87 calories; 20 gm carbohydrate; 2 gm protein; trace fat (4% calories from fat); 1 mg cholesterol; 59 mg sodium; 153 mg potassium; 71 mg caffeine (made with regular coffee).

FAVORITE COFFEE BLENDS

Many specialty and gourmet shops have their own "house" blends. In fact, most of the large roasters make up a house blend. The Coffee Company in Dallas, Texas, was willing to share three of their favorite blends with me.

For all three, mix and blend the beans before grinding. Then, follow any special instructions listed.

JOE'S SAILOR'S BLEND

This is a deep, rich blend with a mellow taste and sharp aftertaste. It makes a great breakfast coffee.

1/4 pound Colombian Supremo (regular or decaffeinated)
1/4 pound Brazilian Santos
2 ounces Viennese Roast
2 ounces French Roast
1/4 pound Celebes Kalossi

JOE'S SPECIAL DESSERT BLEND

This blend may be served topped with whipped cream and a cinnamon stick to stir.

8 ounces Chocolate Almond Coffee
4 ounces Colombian Supremo (regular or decaffeinated)
4 ounces Viennese Cinnamon Coffee

JOE'S TURKISH BLEND

Pulverize (or grind to espresso grind) before brewing in an Ibrik (see recipe on page 63). Or grind to fine grind for use in automatic coffee maker with paper filter.

7-1/2 ounces Ethiopian Mocha Harrar Coffee
8 ounces French Roast Coffee
1/2 ounce ground cardamom

SPECIALTY BLENDS

If your coffee seems to be a little lacking in flavor, try this: add 1/3 part of any of the following coffees.

To add brightness: Costa Rica Coffee
                                 Colombian
                                 Guatemalan

To add body, richness, flavor: Java
                                 Sumatran
                                 Celebes Sulaueise

To add sweetness: Haitian
                                 Indian Mysore

For flavor and aroma: Kona
                                 Jamaican
                                 Mocha

For a winey flavor: Ethiopian
                                 Kenya

Blend with your coffee; grind and brew as for regular coffee.

LOW ACID BLENDS

Good coffee flavor is often accompanied by the acid from certain agents in the coffee. If coffee's acid is troublesome to you, try one of these blends...low in acid, rich in flavor and aroma.

Blend #1:
1/2 pound Java coffee
1/4 pound Sumatran coffee
1/4 pound Brazilian Arabica coffee (expensive)

Blend #2:
1/3 pound Java coffee
1/3 pound Costa Rican coffee
1/3 pound Kenyan coffee

Blend #3:
1/3 pound Colombian coffee
1/3 pound Mexican coffee
1/3 pound Indian Mysore coffee (scarce)

Blend #4:
1/2 pound Colombian coffee
1/4 pound Tanzanian coffee
1/4 pound Kenya AA coffee

50/50

Mike McMahon, a manufacturers' representative in New York City, loves coffee "but the caffeine doesn't love me," says Mike. He suggests using one of the following 50/50 blends.

IRISH CREAM: 50% Irish Cream Regular Coffee/50% Irish Cream Decaffeinated Coffee

AMERICAN BLEND: 50% Costa Rican Coffee/50% Colombia Supremo Decaffeinated Coffee

KING'S BLEND: 50% Kona Coffee/50% Colombian Supremo Decaffeinated Coffee

AFTER DINNER BLEND: 50% French Roast/50% Amaretto Decaffeinated Coffee

AROMATIC BLEND: 50% Kenya AA/ 50% Colombia Supremo Decaffeinated

CONTINENTAL BLEND: 50% Celebes or Tanzania/ 50% Colombia Supremo Decaffeinated Coffee

With each of these, mix beans (or have specialty coffee store mix beans), then grind to a fine grind. Brew as you would for regular coffee. The caffeine will be reduced 50 percent to approximately seventy-five milligrams per cup.

ENGLISH BREAKFAST BLEND COFFEE

**4 ounces
fresh figs
(4-6 figs)**

**1/2 pound
whole bean
Mysore or
Kenya AA or
Ethiopian**

**1/2 pound
whole bean
Colombian
Coffee**

This is the unusual breakfast coffee served in fine English hotels. The unique flavor comes from the combination of roasted figs...and the Mysore (Indian) coffee. Mysore coffee is scarce, and you may replace it with Kenya AA or Ethiopian coffee.

Serves: 32

Wash figs and slice into one-fourth inch slices. Roast at 300° F. until completely dry and crackly. This will take one to two hours. Blend together coffee and figs. Grind and brew as for regular coffee. This blend may be stored in the freezer in a tightly sealed jar for up to two months.

Each serving: 8 calories; 1 gm carbohydrates; trace protein; trace fat; 0 mg cholesterol; 8 mg sodium; 128 mg potassium; 139 mg caffeine (made with regular coffee).

EW ORLEANS BLEND

Chicory is the bitter-tasting cousin of the dandelion. Added to dark roast coffee, it adds a peppery tang to this full-bodied coffee.

Serves: 4

Blend coffee and chicory. Brew as for regular coffee. Serve in warm mugs with hot milk.

Each serving: 28 calories; 3 gm carbohydrates;2 gm protein; 1 gm fat (24% calories from fat); 23 mg cholesterol; 34 mg sodium; 246 mg potassium; 104 mg caffeine (made with regular coffee).

3 tablespoons freshly ground coffee (preferably dark roast)

1 tablespoon ground chicory (available in specialty stores and in some supermarkets)

4, 8-ounce cups cold water

1/2 cup hot milk, 2% milk fat

ROASTING YOUR OWN COFFEE

For the ultimate in fresh coffee flavor, why not roast your own beans? It's easy, as the only equipment you'll need is an expandable steamer. It's important to keep an eye on your coffee as it is roasting, though. Overly roasted coffee beans are flammable.

Preheat oven to 425° F. Spread unroasted, green coffee* beans to a single thickness over an expandable, petal-style vegetable steamer. Carefully place into hot oven. Roast for about ten minutes or until you hear the beans crackling. Coffee is roasted when the beans reach a rich, deep brown. Check every minute or two and remove beans when they have achieved the right color. If any beans spill onto the surface of the oven, clean them up immediately as they are flammable.

Cool roasted beans thoroughly and place them into a jar with a tight fitting top. Store in a dark and dry area. Allow the coffee beans to cure for *two or three days before grinding. Home-roasted coffee beans will retain their flavor for up to four weeks.*

*Unroasted, green coffee beans are available at specialty coffee stores, in some supermarkets, and through coffee roasters.

FLAVORED COFFEES

Flavored coffees combine a whole bean coffee with a powdered or liquid flavoring agent and ground nuts. Each flavored coffee will be a little different...and you may want to try combinations of your own. Please note that the water will go through the grounds a little slower with these coffees.

CHOCOLATE MINT COFFEE

This lightly flavored coffee is excellent as an after dinner coffee. It may also be used in other recipes such as Mocha Mugs (page 67) or South of the Border Coffee Cooler (page 72).

Serves: 16

1/2 pound whole bean coffee

2 tablespoons mint flavoring

1/2 cup unsweetened cocoa

In a small mixing bowl, blend coffee and mint. Place on a baking sheet and bake at 200° F. for one hour. Grind to specifications of coffee maker. Place ground coffee in a medium sized bowl and blend with cocoa powder. Store in a tightly sealed jar in the freezer.

To brew: use one scoop (one tablespoon) coffee for each five ounce cup of water used.

Each serving: 45 calories; 3 gm carbohydrates; 1 gm protein; 4 gm fat (70% calories from fat); 0 mg cholesterol; 8 mg sodium; 188 mg potassium; 147 mg caffeine (made with regular coffee).

CAFE AMARETTO

1/4 pound
sliced almonds

1/2 pound
100% Colombian
coffee (regular or
decaffeinated)

1/4 pound
Italian Roast
Coffee (regular or
decaffeinated)

almond extract

This is a rich, dark coffee with just a hint of almond.

Serves: 32

Place almonds on a baking sheet and roast at 325° F. for 10 minutes or until they are lightly browned. Mix coffee beans and almonds well. When ready to brew, grind to specifications of coffee maker.

Using one tablespoon (or less) coffee for each five-ounce cup, place coffee in coffee filter. To brewing water, add one-half teaspoon almond extract (for eight to twelve cups of coffee). Brew according to manufacturer's directions.

Each serving: 17 calories; 1 gm carbohydrates; trace protein; 1 gm fat (61% calories from fat); 0 mg cholesterol; 6 mg sodium; 109 mg potassium; 104 mg caffeine (made with regular coffee).

ORANGE PECAN COFFEE

Serves: 32

Place pecans on a baking sheet and roast at 325° F. for ten minutes or until they are lightly browned. Mix beans and nuts. When ready to brew, grind to specifications of coffee maker.

Using one tablespoon (or less) coffee for each five ounce cup, place coffee in coffee filter. To brewing water, add one-half teaspoon orange extract (for eight to twelve cups of coffee). Brew according to manufacturer's directions allowing for two to three minutes extra for the water to penetrate the pecan flavored grounds.

1/4 pound pecans

1/2 pound 100% Colombian Coffee (regular or decaffeinated)

1/4 pound Costa Rica Coffee

orange extract

Each serving: 18 calories; 1 gm carbohydrates; trace protein; 1 gm fat (73% calories from fat); 0 mg cholesterol; 6 mg sodium; 102 mg potassium; 104 mg caffeine (made with regular coffee).

COFFEE CONCENTRATE

The ultimate in excellent convenience foods is coffee concentrate. In fact, this is the coffee of preference by farmers in Central America. It will hold its flavor for months if you store it in a tightly capped jug in the refrigerator. It makes an excellent cup of coffee, and is the preferred coffee for cooking. Here are two methods of making coffee concentrate.

HOT WATER COFFEE CONCENTRATE

Hot water coffee concentrate makes a stronger and more distinctive coffee.

Serves: 28

4 cups cold water
1/2 pound finely ground coffee

Brew coffee according to manufacturer's directions. (If your filter won't hold the full half pound, then brew twice using two cups cold water and one-fourth pound of coffee each time). Cool. Store in a glass jug with a tight-fitting seal.

To reconstitute coffee: pour one ounce of hot water coffee concentrate into a warm mug. Fill with boiling water.

COLD WATER CONCENTRATE

If you like a mild, low-acid coffee, this concentrate will work for you.

Serves: 16

4 cups cold water
1/2 pound finely ground coffee

Place water into a two-quart bowl. Stir in coffee so all grounds have been saturated. Cover and place the bowl in a cool, dark corner for ten to twenty hours depending on the strength desired. Line a coffee filter with filter paper and place over a one quart jug with a tight-fitting seal. Pour coffee, a cup at a time, through the filter into the jar. Seal and store in the refrigerator.

To reconstitute: pour one ounce cold concentrate into warm mug. Fill with boiling water.

4 ICED COFFEES

What do you drink when you've had enough hot coffee for the day...when soft drinks seem flat, and when you want a refreshing pick-me-up? I'd suggest an iced coffee. Iced coffee has caffeine for a pick-up (or iced coffee may be prepared with decaffeinated coffee). In addition, these iced coffees have other wonderful ingredients...nutritious banana shakes, delicious coffee coolers with ice creams, and refreshing iced coffees with fruit mixtures.

During hot weather, iced coffee also provides a cooling morning breakfast drink. But, no matter what the weather, I'm sure you'll find that these iced coffee recipes will please coffee lovers. As a matter of fact, some of my non-coffee-drinking friends appreciate the flavors of these iced coffee recipes!

Make sure you brew strong coffee for these recipes. Better still, use one-ounce Hot Coffee Concentrate (page 90) or Cold Coffee Concentrate (page 91) and seven ounces water for each cup of coffee required by these recipes.

AMARETTO ICED COFFEE

1 cup
freshly brewed,
Amaretto coffee
(regular or
decaffeinated)

1 cup milk,
2% milk fat

1/2 teaspoon
pure vanilla
extract

1/3 teaspoon
almond extract

1 tablespoon
granulated sugar

ice cubes

pinch of ground
cinnamon

This coffee has plenty of flavor...yet is light and very refreshing. What a perfect coffee for a hot afternoon!

Serves: 2

Combine the coffee, milk, extracts, and sugar. Place cubes into two tall, twelve ounce glasses. Pour coffee mixture over ice. Sprinkle lightly with ground cinnamon.

Each serving: 72 calories; 8 gm carbohydrate; 4 gm protein; 2 gm fat (30% calories from fat); 9 mg cholesterol; 65 mg sodium; 256 mg potassium; 70 mg caffeine (made with regular coffee).

Banana Frostie

Bananas and coffee...quite a combo. And when you add the ice cream, you'll have a real treat...a lunchtime favorite!

Serves: 2

Cut banana into chunks and combine with coffee and sugar in a blender. Blend at high speed. When mixture is smooth, add ice cream and blend at medium speed until smooth. Pour into two, twelve-ounce glasses.

1 ripe banana

1-1/2 cups cold, strong coffee (regular or decaffeinated)

3 tablespoons granulated sugar

1 cup vanilla ice cream

Each serving: 301 calories; 48 gm carbohydrates; 3 gm protein; 12 gm fat (35% calories from fat); 44 mg cholesterol; 61 mg sodium; 448 mg potassium; 122 mg caffeine (made with regular coffee).

CAFE CHOCOMALT

1 cup cold,
strong coffee
(regular or
decaffeinated)

1 cup milk,
2% milk fat

1 cup chocolate
ice cream

2 tablespoons
granulated
sugar

3 tablespoons
malted-milk
powder

*Here's a great cooler...a coffee malted!
Try this about ten-thirty on a hot, hot
morning!*

Serves: 2

Place all ingredients into blender cup.
Blend at high speed. Serve in tall,
twelve-ounce glasses.

Each serving: 274 calories; 38 gm carbohydrate; 8 gm
protein; 11 gm fat (34% calories from fat); 43 mg
cholesterol; 155 mg sodium; 466 mg potassium; 70 mg
caffeine (made with regular coffee).

Coffee Float

Coffee has a way of blending with ice creams so that it adds a mellow richness. Here's a great beverage...even for those who aren't fond of coffee as a hot beverage.

Serves: 2

Divide the ice cream between two, wide-mouthed, ten-ounce glasses. Divide chocolate syrup and cold coffee between the two glasses. Garnish with whipped cream and candies.

Each serving: 243 calories; 25 gm carbohydrate; 3 gm protein; 31 gm fat (56% calories from fat); 46 mg cholesterol; 67 mg sodium; 241 mg potassium; 76 mg caffeine (made with regular coffee).

1 cup ice cream (vanilla, chocolate, or coffee)

2 tablespoons chocolate syrup

1 cup cold coffee (regular or decaffeinated)

2 tablespoons sweetened whipped cream

1 teaspoon rock candy or other candy sprinkles

COFFEE FROSTIE

1/2 cup
instant nonfat
dry milk

1/2 cup
ice water

1/4 cup
granulated
sugar

1/2 cup strong,
cold coffee
(regular or
decaffeinated)

1 pint coffee
ice cream,
softened

Here's a recipe that will go with breakfast, lunch or dinner. It's light, yet sweet and creamy. It's an especially nice way to use flavored coffees such as Irish Cream Coffee or Amaretto Flavored Coffee.

Serves: 4

Chill beater blades and small bowl of an electric mixer. Measure instant dry milk into chilled bowl. Add ice water; blend. Beat at high speed until soft peaks form (about five minutes). Combine sugar and cold coffee. Add slowly, continuing to beat. Turn to low speed. Add ice cream, about one-quarter of it at time, beating after each addition until blended. Pour into four, ten-ounce stemmed glasses. Serve with sipping straws.

Each serving: 251 calories; 33 gm carbohydrate; 5 gm protein; 12 gm fat (42% calories from fat); 46 mg cholesterol; 101 mg sodium; 272 mg potassium; 18 mg caffeine (made with regular coffee).

CONTINENTAL COFFEE COOLER

When I first tried this recipe, I was thrilled at the way the flavors seemed to sparkle. This is elegant...and has only twenty-five calories per serving!

Serves: 4

Mix together coffee, bitters, vanilla, and sugar. Pour into four, ten-ounce glasses. Add ice cubes to fill within two inches of the top. Top with club soda and orange sections.

Each serving: 25 calories; 6 gm carbohydrate; 0 protein; 0 fat; 0 cholesterol; 28 mg sodium; 73 mg potassium; 51 mg caffeine (made with regular coffee).

1-1/2 cups freshly brewed, French roast coffee

1/2 teaspoon Agnostura bitters

1/2 teaspoon pure vanilla extract

1-1/2 tablespoons sugar

1 cup cold club soda

4 orange sections

COOL COFFEE TROPICANA

4 cups freshly
brewed, French
Roast Coffee

1 cup milk,
2% milk fat

1 teaspoon
rum flavoring

1 tablespoon
simple syrup *

3 cups
cracked ice

1 cup cold
sparkling water
or club soda

This iced coffee is a summertime favorite at Green Mountain Coffee Roasters in Waterbury, Vermont. They sell lots of tall glasses of this cooling confection!

Serves: 6

Combine coffee, milk, rum flavoring, and simple syrup. Chill. Place one-half cup cracked ice in each of six tall glasses. Pour in coffee mixture. Top with sparkling water.

Each serving: 36 calories; 5 gm carbohydrate; 2 gm protein; 1 gm fat (22% calories from fat); 3 mg cholesterol; 38 mg sodium; 165 mg potassium; 75 mg caffeine (made with regular coffee).

*To make simple syrup: simmer one-half cup sugar with one-half cup water for five minutes, until all sugar is dissolved. Cool. Store in a covered jar in the refrigerator. Simple syrup will keep indefinitely. It is a great sweetener for coffee drinks.

I CED CARDAMOM DELIGHT

...another super, low-calorie recipe (under thirty calories). The Scandinavian blend of coffee is wonderful in this recipe. Add pineapple and cherry skewers for a delightful presentation.

Serves: 6

In a saucepan, blend cardamom seeds and water. Bring to a boil and boil for five minutes. Cool water for one hour in refrigerator. Strain water into the water reservoir of coffee maker and brew ground coffee according to manufacturer's directions. Fill six tall, ten-ounce, heat-resistant glasses full of ice. Pour hot coffee over and garnish with pineapple chunks and maraschino cherries which have been skewered onto wooden skewers.

Each serving: 29 calories; 6 gm carbohydrate; 0 protein; .5 gm fat (3% calories from fat); 0 cholesterol; 8 mg sodium; 191 mg potassium; 136 mg caffeine (made with regular coffee).

1 teaspoon cardamom seeds

4 cups cold water

6 scoops (or 6 tablespoons) ground coffee (preferably Scandinavian or Danish blend)

1/2 cup fresh or canned pineapple chunks

18 maraschino cherries

6 wooden skewers, 4 inches long

I CED MOCHA WITH MINT

2 tablespoons
chocolate syrup

3/4 cup freshly
brewed coffee
(regular or
decaffeinated)

1/4 cup milk

dash of
mint extract

1 scoop
crushed ice

mint leaf for
garnish

*This recipe is a great pick-me-up for late
afternoon. It was served to me several
years ago, and I've loved it ever since.
This is written for a single serving but can
be expanded accordingly.*

Serves: 1

In a blender, combine chocolate syrup,
coffee, milk, mint, and crushed ice.
Blend until frothy. Pour into a tall glass
and garnish with a mint leaf and straw.

Each serving: 123 calories; 26 gm carbohydrate; 3 gm
protein; 2 gm fat (11% calories from fat); 5 mg cholesterol; 62 mg sodium; 319 mg potassium; 102 mg caffeine
(made with regular coffee).

I CED SLENDERELLA

This is a basic iced coffee recipe. It is refreshing, low in calories, and extremely easy to prepare.

Serves: 4

Fill blender cup half full of ice cubes. Add coffee and sugar. Blend until thick and foamy. Pour into four tall glasses.

Each serving: 29 calories; 7 gm carbohydrate; 0 protein; 0 gm fat; 0 cholesterol; 6 mg sodium; 102 mg potassium; 51 mg caffeine (made with regular coffee).

ice cubes

1-1/2 cups strong, cool coffee (regular or decaffeinated)

1 tablespoon granulated sugar

ICED TOFFEE

1 Heath Bar, 1-3/16 ounces
2 cups vanilla ice cream
1/2 cup cold, strong coffee (regular or decaffeinated)

Here's a great recipe for anyone who loves toffee. This is the perfect dessert beverage.

Serves: 2

Break Heath Bar into four pieces. Place in blender cup with softened ice cream and coffee. Blend on high until candy is blended smooth and the mixture is thick. Pour into two, twelve-ounce glasses. Serve with a spoon.

Each serving: 448 calories; 39 gm carbohydrate; 7 gm protein; 31 gm fat (60% calories from fat); 88 mg cholesterol; 119 mg sodium; 341 mg potassium; 34 mg caffeine (made with regular coffee).

I CY JAVA MINT

This is a drink for mint lovers. It is cooling, refreshing...yet a very different kind of treat. Try this after a light, salad luncheon on a hot, hot day.

Serves: 4

Mix together coffee, simple syrup, half and half, and mint extract. Divide into four, ten-ounce glasses which are partially filled with crushed ice. Top with whipped cream and a mint sprig.

Each serving: 111 calories; 15 gm carbohydrate; 1 gm protein; 5 gm fat (42% calories from fat); 17 mg cholesterol; 30 mg sodium; 186 mg potassium; 136 mg caffeine (made with regular coffee).

4 cups cold coffee (regular or decaffeinated)

1/2 cup simple syrup (page 102)

1/2 cup half and half

1/2 teaspoon mint extract

2 cups crushed ice

1/2 cup sweetened whipped cream

mint sprigs for garnish

I CY JAZZBERRY JAVA

1 package frozen
raspberries
(10 ounces)

1/2 cup
granulated
sugar

1/2 cup water

10 cups cold
coffee (regular
or decaffeinated)

1 pint half
and half

1 cup sweetened
whipped cream

10 mint sprigs

10 whole
raspberries

*Green Mountain Coffee Roasters in Water-
bury, Vermont, like to create coffees with
appeal to college students. When my son,
Bob, was in college at The University of
Vermont, this was practically his favorite
beverage.*

Serves: 10

Puree frozen raspberries, sugar, and water
in a blender cup. Strain mixture into a
large mixing bowl. Add coffee and half
and half. Blend well. Ladle into ten,
twelve-ounce glasses partially filled with
cracked ice. Top with whipped cream,
mint sprigs, and whole raspberries.

Each serving: 155 calories; 22 gm carbohydrate; 2 gm
protein; 7 gm fat (40% calories from fat); 23 mg
cholesterol; 36 mg sodium; 247 mg potassium; 136 mg
caffeine (made with regular coffee).

MIDNIGHT SUN COOLER

During the first year's business at Village Roaster, in Lakewood, Colorado, Mary Ann and Gary Mencimer were looking for ways to stimulate coffee sales during the heat of the summer. This recipe was a hit!

Serves: 2

Chill freshly made coffee. Rapidly froth all ingredients (except strawberries) in blender. Serve in chilled Irish coffee glasses garnished with a strawberry on the rim of the glass.

Each serving: 190 calories; 26 gm carbohydrate; 3 gm protein; 8 gm fat (39% calories from fat); 30 mg cholesterol; 74 mg sodium; 400 mg potassium; 280 mg caffeine (made with regular coffee).

2 cups Scandinavian Blend (or Danish Blend) Coffee, brewed double strength

1 teaspoon pure Dutch cocoa

1 teaspoon vanilla extract

4 teaspoons sugar

4 ice cubes

1 cup vanilla ice cream

2 strawberries for garnish

MOCHA MIST

2-1/2 cups
strong, cold
coffee
(regular or
decaffeinated)

5 tablespoons
chocolate syrup

1 pint coffee
ice cream

Here's a frosty beverage which may just be better than a milk shake. It's rich and chocolatey.

Serves: 4

Place all ingredients in blender and blend until smooth. Pour into four tall glasses.

Each serving: 231 calories; 31 gm carbohydrate; 3 gm protein; 12 gm fat (45% calories from fat); 44 mg cholesterol; 72 mg sodium; 261 mg potassium; 155 mg caffeine (made with regular coffee).

Mocha Silk Soda

Is this a dessert...or an iced coffee? Either way, you'll spoon this satiny smooth cooler at the beginning, but you'll end up by sipping it through a straw! To reduce calories, Mocha Silk Soda may be made with frozen yogurt or ice milk.

Serves: 4

Ladle one scoop (one-half cup) of each ice cream into four, large, heat-proof soda glasses. Pour one cup hot coffee over each glass. Top with whipped cream.

Each serving (made with ice cream): 550 calories; 50 gm carbohydrate; 6 gm protein; 37 gm fat (60% calories from fat); 137 mg cholesterol; 179 mg sodium; 478 mg potassium; 136 mg caffeine (made with regular coffee).

1 pint chocolate ice cream

1 pint vanilla ice cream

1 pint coffee ice cream

4 cups freshly brewed, hot coffee (regular or decaffeinated)

1/2 cup sweetened whipped cream

Mock de Menthe

1 cup cold, strong coffee (regular or decaffeinated)

1 cup vanilla ice cream

1 cup mint ice cream

1 teaspoon mint extract

mint leaves for garnish

This tastes like a grasshopper...smooth, and mellow. Yet, this version has that secret ingredient, COFFEE!

Serves: 4

Place coffee, ice creams, and mint extract into blender cup. Blend until smooth. Pour into four champagne or wine glasses. Top with mint leaves.

Each serving: 176 calories; 16 gm carbohydrate; 2 gm protein; 12 gm fat (59% calories from fat); 44 mg cholesterol; 56 mg sodium; 144 mg potassium; 35 mg caffeine (made with regular coffee).

PEANUT BUTTER - JELLY FLOAT

This drink has a smooth, delicious, nutty flavor with just a hint of sweetness for the kid inside us all.

Serves: 2

Place all ingredients in a blender cup. Blend at high speed until foamy. Pour into two, eight-ounce glasses.

Each serving: 220 calories; 34 gm carbohydrates; 7 gm protein; 7 gm fat (26% calories from fat); 10 mg cholesterol; 120 mg sodium; 374 mg potassium; 70 mg caffeine (made with regular coffee).

1 cup cold, strong coffee (regular or decaffeinated)

1 cup milk, 2% milk fat

1 heaping tablespoon smooth style peanut butter

4 tablespoons strawberry jelly

SPICY ICED COFFEE

3 cups
freshly brewed,
Mexican coffee

2 cinnamon
sticks

4 cloves

4 allspice
berries

lemon peel
for garnish

Try using Mexican Grown Coffee for this iced treat. The flavors blend well...a real must for iced coffee lovers!

Serves: 4

Pour coffee over cinnamon sticks, cloves, and allspice berries. Let stand for one hour. Pour mixture over ice which has been divided between four tall glasses. Garnish with lemon peel.

Each serving: 10 calories; trace gm carbohydrates; 0 gm protein; 0 gm fat; 0 mg cholesterol; 0 mg sodium; 0 mg potassium; 122 mg caffeine (made with regular coffee).

TROPICAL MOCHA SMOOTHIE

Here's a great way to have breakfast in a glass. It's creamy, flavorful, and only 166 calories per serving.

Serves: 2

Combine first four ingredients into a blender cup. Blend until smooth and creamy. Pour over crushed ice into a tall cooler glass. Garnish with chocolate curls and serve with a straw.

Each serving: 166 calories; 32 gm carbohydrate; 6 gm protein; 3 gm fat (15% calories from fat); 10 mg cholesterol; 85 mg sodium; 546 mg potassium; 37 mg caffeine (made with regular coffee).

1 ripe banana

1 cup milk, 2% milk fat

2 tablespoons chocolate syrup

1/2 cup cold coffee

chocolate curls for garnish

CAFE MAZAGRAN

1 cup
crushed ice

1/2 cup cool,
strong brewed
coffee, prefera-
bly Mexican or
Costa Rican
(regular or
decaffeinated)

1 teaspoon
simple syrup
(page 102)

1/2 cup cold
club soda

*A very refreshing beverage, this is best
made with a Latin American coffee such
as Mexican or Costa Rican.*

Serves: 1

Fill a twelve-ounce glass with crushed ice.
Add coffee and stir in syrup. Slowly pour
in club soda.

Each serving: 12 calories; 2 gm carbohydrate; 0 gm
protein; 0 gm fat; 0 mg cholesterol; 28 mg sodium; 64
mg potassium; 70 mg caffeine (made with regular coffee).

S PICED CITRUS ICED COFFEE

This full-flavored coffee will become even spicier as it cures in the refrigerator.

Serves: 6

Place lemon strip, orange strip, and cloves into a coffee carafe. Brew coffee according to manufacturers' directions.   Cool and store in a sealed jug in the refrigerator for twelve hours. To serve: add simple syrup, half and half and pour into six tall, twelve-ounce glasses.

Each serving: 24 calories; 2 gm carbohydrate; trace protein; 1 gm fat (50% calories from fat); 4 mg cholesterol; 9 mg sodium; 98 mg potassium; 93 mg caffeine (made with regular coffee).

1 strip, 2 by 1/2 inch, lemon peel

1 strip, 4 by 1/2 inch, orange peel

12 whole cloves

4 tablespoons light roast coffee such as Colombian (regular or decaffeinated)

4 cups water

4 teaspoons simple syrup (page 102)

4 tablespoons half and half

SMOOTH AND CREAMY ICED CAFE

1 cup strong, cold coffee (regular or decaffeinated)

4 teaspoons confectioners' sugar

1 cup half and half

3 cups crushed ice

Call this a creamy slush with a milk coffee flavor. Or, just call it delicious.

Serves: 4

Place all ingredients into a blender cup. Blend until smooth. Pour into four, ten-ounce glasses.

Each serving: 89 calories; 5 gm carbohydrate; 2 gm protein; 7 gm fat (70% calories from fat); 22 mg cholesterol; 27 mg sodium; 111 mg potassium; 35 mg caffeine (made with regular coffee).

5 ESPRESSO AND CAPPUCCINO

If flavored and specialty coffees were the beverages of the '80s, then espresso and cappuccino are truly the beverages of the '90s. The rich flavor of espresso and the smooth taste of cappuccino are perfect afternoon pick-ups.

Perhaps none of the coffee beverages are as misunderstood as the names of these beverages. It's really very simple. Espresso is finely ground, dark-roast coffee which has been made under pressure and steam. Cappuccino, on the other hand, is espresso with richly steamed milk.

Contrary to popular opinion, the deeply roasted coffees used for espresso actually have less caffeine than lighter-roasted coffee. If caffeine is a consideration, you may also purchase decaffeinated espresso coffee. It is very important to grind the coffee to an espresso grind so that it will work properly with your espresso-making equipment.

By very lenient Italian standards, one may put a lump of sugar and a twist of lemon into espresso, but that's as far as the rules will bend. In *my versions of these Italian favorites, however, we've gone beyond tradition. You'll find some espresso and cappuccino recipes which do not require a special machine, or espresso maker and are exceptionally delicious.*

AUTHENTIC ESPRESSO OR CAPPUCCINO

For this recipe, you'll need an electric or top-of-the-stove espresso maker. On page 120, you'll see a photo of the authentic espresso maker given to me by son, Bob, during his year-long art history study in Florence, Italy. His Italian family used one like this on a daily basis.

Serves: 2

Put two espresso-sized cups cold water into the reservoir of an espresso machine. Lock the reservoir. Place the espresso coffee into the filter and snap the filter into place. Turn on machine. Espresso will brew in two and one-half to four minutes. Serve hot, in small cups. If desired, serve with a sugar cube or lemon twist.

2, 2-1/2 espresso sized cups of water (use larger amount for Cappuccino)

1 tablespoon finely ground espresso coffee

1/2 cup cold milk, 2% milk fat (for cappuccino)

2 sugar cubes (optional)

2 lemon twists (optional)

FOR CAPPUCCINO: use the larger amount of water and place in reservoir. Follow the above recipe. When unit begins to brew espresso coffee, place steam nozzle of unit into the top one-half inch of the pitcher of cold milk. Allow the steam to froth and bubble the milk for a full one minute. Milk will expand to fill the pitcher and will be hot with a dry froth. Spoon froth from the milk onto the cups of espresso. Serve immediately.

Each serving (cappuccino): 46 calories; 2 gm carbohydrates; 6 gm protein; 1 gm fat (25% calories from fat); 5 mg cholesterol; 40 mg sodium; 177 mg potassium; 70 mg caffeine (made with regular coffee).

BRANDIED CAPPUCCINO

1 cup half & half

2 small cups
freshly-brewed
espresso coffee
(regular or decaf.)

1 tablespoon
honey

1 tspn. cocoa
(unsweetened)

3/4 tspn. vanilla

2 tablespoons
brandy

2 tablespoons
Kahlua (or other
coffee liqueur)

1 tablespoon
light rum

1 tablespoon
Galliano

1/2 cup sweet-
ened whipped
cream

shaved chocolate

*Cappuccino goes well with liqueurs.
Here's a very powerful combination. If
you want to reduce the alcohol and
calorie content, simply boil liqueurs for
about ten minutes. Add to espresso, pour
into heat-proof glasses and top with
whipped cream.*

Serves: 4

Whisk half and half, espresso, honey,
cocoa, and vanilla in a two-quart saucepan. Heat until almost scalded. Add
brandy, Kahlua, rum and Galiano and
pour into four Irish whiskey (or other
heat-proof wine) glasses. Garnish with
whipped cream and shaved chocolate.

Each serving: 263 calories; 14 gm carbohydrates; 3 gm
protein; 17 gm fat (57% calories from fat); 55 mg
cholesterol; 38 mg sodium; 153 mg potassium; 36 mg
caffeine (made with regular coffee); 19% calories from
alcohol.

CAFE KEITH

...an adaptation from Rick's Cafe in Indianapolis, Indiana.

Serves: 2

Combine brewed espresso with brandy and Frangelico. Pour into two large, demitasse cups. Top with whipped cream; place a cinnamon stick into each.

Each serving: 133 calories; 4 gm carbohydrate; 1 gm protein; 9 gm fat (63% calories from fat); 33 mg cholesterol; 15 mg sodium; 93 mg potassium; 70 mg caffeine (made with regular coffee); 23% calories from alcohol.

2 small cups freshly brewed espresso (regular or decaffeinated)

1 tablespoon brandy (or Grand Marnier)

1 tablespoon Frangelico

1/4 cup sweetened whipped cream

2 cinnamon sticks (for stirring)

CAFE BORGATTA

1 cup milk,
2% milk fat

2 tablespoons
unsweetened
cocoa

2 tablespoons
granulated
sugar

2 small cups
freshly brewed
espresso
(regular or
decaffeinated)

1/2 cup sweet-
ened whipped
cream

grated orange

*Here's a rich and satisfying drink ...
perhaps it's the mocha of the '90s.*

Serves: 4

Heat milk in a small saucepan. Sift cocoa
and sugar into milk and whisk to blend.
Stir in espresso. Divide equally into four
small espresso or demitasse cups. Top
with whipped cream and grated orange.

Each serving: 116 calories; 13 gm carbohydrate; 3 gm
protein; 7 gm fat (48% calories from fat); 11 mg
cholesterol; 50 mg sodium; 250 mg potassium; 77 mg
caffeine (made with regular coffee).

Café Latte

...this is the Italian version of Cafe au Lait. In Italy, if you go to the espresso counter and stand while ordering and drinking your Cafe Latte, you'll save several thousand lira!

Serves: 4

Steam milk with steam nozzle of espresso maker. To froth this quantity of milk, you may also place hot milk into a blender cup and blend on highest speed for ten seconds. When milk is frothy, pour most of milk into four, warm, eight-ounce mugs. Next, pour coffee down sides of mugs. Spoon froth from milk over coffee and sprinkle with cinnamon. Serve with one cube of sugar.

2 cups milk,
2% milk fat

2 cups freshly
brewed, hot
espresso
(regular or
decaffeinated)

ground
cinnamon

4 cubes sugar

Each serving: 80 calories; 9 gm carbohydrate; 5 gm protein; 2 gm fat (28% calories from fat); 10 mg cholesterol; 77 mg sodium; 291 mg potassium; 70 mg caffeine (made with regular coffee).

CAPPUCCINO BLANCO

Do you like a lighter version of espresso? Maybe the espresso flavor with a little added sweetness and flavor? Then, this cappuccino is for you. It's light and sweet with a hint of vanilla.

Serves: 2

In a small saucepan, combine the milk and vanilla. Scald the milk. Remove from heat. Cover and let the milk steep for five minutes.

Next, stir sugar into the milk. Reheat briefly and remove the vanilla bean.

Transfer the milk to a blender. Whirl milk until frothy, at least forty-five seconds. Half fill two warmed, eight-ounce coffee mugs with hot espresso coffee. Add the hot milk; sprinkle with cinnamon.

1/2 cup milk, 2% milk fat

1 vanilla bean, split

1 teaspoon light brown sugar

2 servings (6 ounces total) freshly brewed, espresso (regular or decaffeinated)

ground cinnamon

Each serving: 51 calories; 6 gm carbohydrate; 2 gm protein; 1 gm fat (24% calories from fat); 5 mg cholesterol; 45 mg sodium; 255 mg potassium; 139 mg caffeine (made with regular coffee).

FROSTY MINTED MOCHA

2 tablespoons
chocolate
syrup

2 small cups
freshly brewed
espresso coffee
(regular or
decaffeinated)

2 ounces milk,
2% milk fat

1 teaspoon
mint extract

crushed ice

2 mint leaves

*This light, tasty espresso is the perfect
ending to dinner on a hot night. It's easy
to prepare, and you may use hot or cold
espresso.*

Serves: 2

In a blender, combine chocolate syrup,
coffee, milk, mint extract, and crushed
ice. Blend until frothy. Pour into a ten-
ounce glass and garnish with a mint leaf.

Each serving: 65 calories; 13 gm carbohydrate; 1 gm
protein; 1 gm fat (10% calories from fat); 1 mg cholesterol; 35 mg sodium; 240 mg potassium; 141 mg caffeine
(made with regular coffee).

I CED ELEGANTISSIMO

This is the ultimate. Make it in advance, then watch as your guests rave over this sweet, chocolate delight. It's worth every one of its calories.

Serves: 4

Stir the hot espresso, sugar, and chocolate together until the sugar dissolves and the chocolate melts. Refrigerate until well chilled, three hours or overnight.

Fill wine glasses with finely crushed ice. Pour the cold coffee over the ice. Whisk the cream until just thick enough to mound onto a spoon. Place a spoonful on each glass. Top with chocolate shavings and serve with a straw.

Each serving: 180 calories; 29 gm carbohydrate; 1 gm protein; 8 gm fat (38% calories from fat); 20 mg cholesterol; 10 mg sodium; 102 mg potassium; 74 mg caffeine (made with regular coffee).

2 small cups freshly brewed espresso (regular or decaffeinated)

1/2 cup superfine granulated sugar

1 square (1 ounce) semi-sweet chocolate, chopped

2 cups finely crushed ice

1/4 cup heavy cream

chocolate shavings for garnish

MICROWAVE CAPPUCCINO

1 cup vanilla
ice cream

4 microwave-
proof wine
glasses (or Irish
coffee glasses),
8 ounces each

4 cups Italian
Espresso Coffee
(regular or
decaffeinated)
brewed in a
regular coffee
maker (use a
paper filter)

This faux recipe is fun. It is also quick, delicious, and has quite the authentic flavor. It was given to me by my friend, Lila Greenberg, who lives in the San Francisco Bay Area.

Serves: 4

Scoop one-fourth cup ice cream into each glass. Microwave until ice cream is warm and bubbled up into the cup, one and one-half to two minutes (for all four glasses). Add brewed espresso.

Each serving: 95 calories; 9 gm carbohydrate; 1 gm protein; 6 gm fat (58% calories from fat); 22 mg cholesterol; 35 mg sodium; 191 mg potassium; 139 mg caffeine (made with regular coffee).

Mocha Fino

Here's a mocha with a subtle, espresso flavor...it's a dream!

Serves: 2

Into two, ten-ounce mugs, pour espresso, sugar and cocoa powder. Heat cream; divide between two mugs. Sprinkle with chocolate shavings.

Each serving: 267 calories; 10 gm carbohydrate; 3 gm protein; 24 gm fat (80% calories from fat; 80 mg cholesterol; 56 mg sodium; 297 mg potassium; 141 mg caffeine (made with regular coffee).

2 small cups freshly-brewed espresso (regular or decaffeinated)

2 teaspoons sugar

1 teaspoon unsweetened cocoa powder

1 cup half and half

shaved chocolate

6 COFFEE WITH SPIRITS

Coffee makes a great ending to a meal. And the recipes in this chapter will enhance and enchant your guests. Whether it's an intimate party for two or a dinner party for twelve, your guests will enjoy coffee with spirits.

You'll notice we've added a new figure to the nutrition analysis for this chapter: percentage of calories from alcohol. These recipes are delicious and different. So, if you don't need to count calories, enjoy.

If you are like some of us, though, you'll want to know how many calories you are consuming with that dessert cup of coffee.   One of the easiest ways to reduce the calories in any of these spirited recipes is to boil the alcohol before adding to the coffee. In this way, you'll remove almost all of the alcohol and with it the calories.

In addition, you may want to use decaffeinated coffee for these recipes.   If you do plan to use decaf, I would suggest you start with a decaffeinated Colombia Supremo, then add French roast decaf, and Espresso decaf to your collection.

So, here's to the spirit of coffee drinking while drinking coffee with spirits!

BLACK BEAUTY

...a recipe for brandy lovers!

Serves: 1

Place cracked ice into a large, heat-proof brandy snifter. Pour ingredients over and stir.

Each serving: 171 calories; 5 gm carbohydrates; 0 protein; 0 gm fat; 0 cholesterol; 4 mg sodium; 136 mg potassium; 64 mg caffeine (made with regular coffee); 89% calories from alcohol.

1 ounce brandy

1 ounce dark rum, 100 proof

4 ounces black coffee (regular or decaffeinated)

2 teaspoons powdered sugar

BRANDIED COFFEE PUNCH

6 eggs

grated peel of one lemon

1/2 cup granulated sugar

3 cups cold, strong coffee (regular or decaffeinated)

2/3 cup brandy or cognac

This is a holiday punch, served at Christmas in Denmark. My recipe comes to me via New Orleans and Phyllis Jordan's PJ's Coffee & Tea Co., Inc. This is sweet, creamy, delicious.

Serves: 6

Beat eggs and lemon peel until mixture is light and fluffy. Add sugar a little at a time, beating continuously. Continue beating until thick. Slowly stir in the coffee and then add brandy or cognac.

Serve in chilled glasses.

Each serving: 211 calories; 17 gm carbohydrate; 6 gm protein; 6 gm fat (24% calories from fat); 274 mg cholesterol; 73 mg sodium; 133 mg potassium; 70 mg caffeine (made with regular coffee); 33 % calories from alcohol.

BRANDY FROSTED

The flavors of brandy and coffee here are subtly blended with the richness of cream. This coffee is delicious with or without brandy.

Serves: 2

In blender cup, place sugar, ice cubes, and coffee. Blend for twenty seconds on medium. Remove cap and add half and half and brandy. Blend for five seconds. Pour iced coffee into two, tall glasses. Top with sweetened whipped cream.

Each serving: 456 calories; 24 gm carbohydrate; 7 gm protein; 29 mg fat (58% calories from fat); 95 mg cholesterol; 115 mg sodium; 461 mg potassium; 139 mg caffeine (made with regular coffee);15% calories from alcohol.

2 tablespoons granulated sugar

4 ice cubes

1 cup cold, strong, black coffee (regular or decaffeinated)

1 cup half and half

2 ounces brandy (or Grand Marnier)

1/4 cup sweetened whipped cream

CAFE AU VIN

1 cup cold
strong French
roast coffee
(regular or
decaffeinated)

2 ounces
Tawny Port

2 tablespoons
granulated
sugar

1/2 teaspoon
grated orange
peel

dash of
cinnamon

*You don't often think of serving coffee
with wine. Tawny port has the body and
flavor to make a nice marriage with
French roast coffee. We think you'll
appreciate this as a great dinner coffee.*

Serves: 2

Combine ingredients and mix in a
blender cup at high speed. Pour into
chilled wine glasses.

Each serving: 94 calories; 16 gm carbohydrate; 0 protein;
0 gm fat; 0 cholesterol; 5 mg sodium; 89 mg potassium;
70 mg caffeine (made with regular coffee); 31% calories
from alcohol.

CAFE FLAMBE

This is a dramatic, yet simple and fun idea-recipe.

Serves: 2

Soak a cube of sugar in brandy for ten minutes. Place into a teaspoon and hold so that it will rest on top of the cup of coffee. Ignite. Hold until flame burns out and drop contents into the coffee.

2 sugar cubes

2 teaspoons brandy or cognac

2 cups hot coffee (regular or decaffeinated)

Each serving: 12 calories; 3 gm carbohydrate; 0 protein; 0 fat (no calories from fat); 0 cholesterol; 8 mg sodium; 139 mg caffeine (made with regular coffee); no calories from alcohol as it has burned out!

Cafe Jamaica

2 ounces
Kahlua (or
coffee liqueur)

2 ounces dark
rum, 100 proof

2 cups strong,
hot coffee
(regular or
decaffeinated)

1/4 cup
sweetened
whipped cream

nutmeg (for
garnish)

Here's a great hot coffee with a tropical twist. It's also great when poured over crushed ice.

Serves: 2

Place Kahlua and rum into two, heat-proof coffee mugs. Add coffee. Stir. Top with whipped cream and nutmeg.

Each serving: 270 calories; 13 gm carbohydrate; 1 gm protein; 9 gm fat (31% calories from fat); 33 mg cholesterol; 15 mg sodium; 94 mg potassium; 69 mg caffeine (made with regular coffee); 49% calories from alcohol.

CAMPFIRE CAFE

Here's a recipe from a good friend in Dallas, Texas, Ron Weunsch. Ron is an avid hunter who likes a warm campfire, close friends, and Campfire Cafe on a brisk fall evening.

Serves: 6

Peel orange into one, long peel. Do the same with lemon. Stud each long peel with cloves (eight each). Over campfire, heat water in a large, open pan. When water is boiling, add coffee and allow to boil for five minutes. When time is up, add one more cup cold water to settle out grounds.

In second pan, heat studded orange and lemon peels, sugar cubes, and cinnamon pieces until sugar melts. Add strained, hot coffee to mixture. Slightly warm cognac or brandy. Ignite. Holding orange and lemon peels with heat-proof tongs, slowly pour burning brandy down peels into hot coffee. Strain again and serve in large mugs.

1 orange

1 lemon

16 cloves

1 quart plus 1 cup very cold water

6 tablespoons French Market Coffee (coffee with chicory)

8 sugar cubes

8 cinnamon pieces, 1 inch each

8 ounces brandy or cognac

Each serving: 18 calories; 3 carbohydrates; 0 protein; 0 gm fat; 0 cholesterol; 8 mg sodium; 136 mg potassium; 139 mg caffeine (made with regular coffee); no calories from alcohol as it burned out.

CAFE SEVILLE

This is a refreshing beverage to serve with salads or desserts. It is frothy, with just a tang from citrus and Cointreau.

Serves: 2

Place all ingredients except orange slices into a blender cup and blend at a high speed until frothy. Divide between two, sixteen-ounce glasses. Garnish with orange slices.

Each serving: 229 calories; 32 gm carbohydrate; 5 gm protein; 2 gm fat (9% calories from fat); 10 mg cholesterol; 81 mg sodium; 400 mg potassium; 139 mg caffeine (made with regular coffee); 28% calories from alcohol.

**1/2 cup
chopped ice**

**2 cups strong,
cold coffee
(regular or
decaffeinated)**

**2 tablespoons
granulated
sugar**

**1/4 cup
Cointreau**

**1/4 teaspoon
grated orange
peel**

**1 cup milk,
2% milk fat**

2 slices orange

CHOCOLATE GRASSHOPPER

1 cup strong, cold coffee (regular or decaffeinated)

1 cup chocolate ice cream

2 ounces white creme de menthe

4 mint sprigs for garnish

Here's a lovely dessert coffee. Serve it in wide-mouthed champagne glasses with a straw and pizzelle cookies.

Serves: 4

Mix all ingredients in blender cup. Blend at low speed. Pour into four, wide-mouthed champagne or wine glasses. Garnish with mint sprig.

Each serving: 141 calories; 14 gm carbohydrate; 1 gm protein; 6 gm fat (37% calories from fat); 22 mg cholesterol; 30 mg sodium; 89 mg potassium; 35 mg caffeine (made with regular coffee); 21 % calories from alcohol.

DANISH COFFEE

Here's an interesting way to clarify your coffee.

Serves: 2

Place a clean dime in the bottom of both coffee cups. Cover with coffee until it is no longer visible. Now, pour liqueur into the cup until the coin appears again. (Don't drink the dime!)

Each serving: 170 calories; 1 gm carbohydrate; 0 protein; 0 gm fat; 0 cholesterol; 8 mg sodium; 136 mg potassium; 139 mg caffeine (made with regular coffee); 97% calories from alcohol.

2 small demitasse cups

2 ounces hot, strong coffee (regular or decaffeinated)

2 ounces aquavit or kummel (caraway liqueur)

Devil's Delight

2 cups freshly
brewed French
roast coffee
(regular or
decaffeinated)

4 tablespoons
Kahlua (or
coffee liqueur)

1 tablespoon
creme de cacao

1 cup whipping
cream, whipped

4 tablespoonfuls
chocolate
syrup

Devilishly rich...with more than a hint of Kahlua.

Serves: 4

Blend together coffee, Kahlua, and creme de cacao. Pour into four, heat-proof parfait glasses, eight ounces each. Top each with one-fourth cup whipped cream. Dot with chocolate syrup dots to resemble chocolate chips.

Each serving: 285 calories; 12 gm carbohydrate; 1 gm protein; 22 gm fat (68% calories from fat); 82 mg cholesterol; 30 mg sodium; 130 mg potassium; 70 mg caffeine (made with regular coffee); 14% calories from alcohol.

IRISH COFFEE

...the traditional recipe.

Serves: 6

In a chilled bowl, beat whipping cream with sugar and vanilla until firm. In six Irish whiskey glasses (or eight-ounce, heat-proof wine glasses), pour one ounce Irish whiskey, a tablespoon of brown sugar and coffee. Stir. Gently place whipped cream on coffee. Serve immediately.

Each serving: 281 calories; 19 gm carbohydrate; 1 gm protein; 15 gm fat (41% calories from fat); 54 mg cholesterol; 27 mg sodium; 213 mg potassium; 139 mg caffeine (made with regular coffee); 33% calories from alcohol.

1/2 pint whipping cream

2 tablespoons granulated sugar

1 teaspoon vanilla extract

6 ounces Irish whiskey

6 tablespoons brown sugar

6 cups freshly brewed French roast coffee (regular or decaffeinated)

IRISH COFFEE (NO LIQUOR)

1 cup strong, hot coffee (regular or decaffeinated)

1 tablespoon orange juice

1 teaspoon lemon juice

2 tablespoons sweetened whipped cream

This has the authentic Irish coffee flavor...without the alcohol!

Serves: 1

Pour hot coffee into an eight-ounce, heat-proof wine glass or Irish whiskey glass. Add orange juice and lemon juice. Stir. Top with whipped cream.

Each serving: 35 calories; 4 gm carbohydrate; 0 protein; 2 gm fat (48% calories from fat); 6 mg cholesterol; 18 mg sodium; 184 mg potassium; 139 mg caffeine (made with regular coffee).

I TALIAN COFFEE

This unusual recipe is an innovative way to complete an Italian meal. It is light and satisfying.

Serves: 2

Divide Amaretto into two, heat-resistant wine glasses or mugs. Fill with coffee. Top each coffee with one-half scoop of ice cream and a sprinkle of coriander.

Each serving: 231 calories; 22 gm carbohydrate; 1 gm protein; 6 gm fat (23% calories from fat); 22 mg cholesterol; 35 mg sodium; 219 mg potassium; 139 mg caffeine; 38% calories from alcohol.

3 ounces Amaretto liqueur

2 cups Italian roast coffee (regular or decaffeinated)

1 scoop coffee ice cream

ground coriander

ITALIAN COFFEE II

**1 pint
whipping cream**

**2 ounces
Galliano (or
Neopolitan)
liqueur**

**4 cups French
or Italian roast
coffee (regular or
decaffeinated)**

Another great, rich Italian coffee!

Serves: 4

Whip cream with liqueur until firm. Pour coffee into four, heat-proof wine glasses. Top with whipped cream.

Each serving: 258 calories; 7 gm carbohydrate; 1 gm protein; 22 gm fat (76% calories from fat); 82 mg cholesterol; 30 mg sodium; 180 mg potassium; 139 mg caffeine (made with regular coffee); 11% calories from alcohol.

ITALIAN COFFEE III

...still a different twist on Italian coffee.

Serves: 4

Blend Amaretto and rum; divide between four, heat-proof wine glasses. Pour in coffee. Stir. Float heavy cream on top.

Each serving: 150 calories; 6 gm carbohydrate; 0 protein; 6 gm fat (29% calories from fat); 20 mg cholesterol; 14 mg sodium; 147 mg potassium; 139 mg caffeine (made with regular coffee); 56% calories from alcohol.

2 ounces
Amaretto
liqueur

2 ounces
dark rum

4 cups strong,
hot coffee
(regular or
decaffeinated)

4 tablespoons
heavy cream

MEXICAN COFFEE

2 ounces
Kahlua (or
coffee liqueur)

1 ounce Tequila

2 cups strong,
hot coffee
(preferably
Mexican Coffee)

1/4 cup
whipped cream

ground
cinnamon

Mexican food is great at Luchita's in Cleveland with wonderful Mexican coffee. Here is an adaptation of their recipe.

Serves: 2

Pour Kahlua and tequila into a coffee mug. Add coffee. Stir. Top with whipped cream and cinnamon.

Each serving: 233 calories; 24 gm carbohydrate; 1 gm protein; 9 gm fat (36% calories from fat); 33 mg cholesterol; 19 mg sodium; 158 mg potassium; 140 mg caffeine (made with regular coffee); 40% calories from alcohol.

Mocha Rum Punch

Anna Turner Mysenbery is a food editor in south Florida. She writes that this recipe is "southern party fare."

Serves: 12

Whip cream with sugar and vanilla until it is firm. Blend in ice cream. Combine with coffee and rum. Pour into a twelve-cup punch bowl. Stir until smooth. Serve immediately.

Each serving: 146 calories; 7 gm carbohydrate; 1 gm protein; 11 gm fat (65% calories from fat); 42 mg cholesterol; 28 mg sodium; 97 mg potassium; 46 mg caffeine (made with regular coffee); 13% calories from alcohol.

1 cup whipping cream

1 tablespoon granulated sugar

1 teaspoon pure vanilla extract

1 pint chocolate ice cream, cut into 2-inch chunks

1/4 cup dark rum (more, if desired)

4 cups freshly brewed coffee (regular or decaffeinated)

SPICED COFFEE BRACER

2 cups cold, strong coffee (regular or decaffeinated)

2 ounces light rum

2 tablespoons granulated sugar

2 tablespoons light cream

dash powdered cloves

dash allspice

2 cinnamon sticks

Be sure to try this great cocktail coffee. It's spicy, refreshing, and light.

Serves: 2

Fill two twelve-ounce tall drink glasses with ice cubes. Add coffee, rum, sugar, cream, cloves, and allspice. Stir. Garnish with cinnamon sticks.

Each serving: 107 calories; 5 gm carbohydrate; 1 gm protein; 2 gm fat (15% calories from fat); 6 mg cholesterol; 14 mg sodium; 155 mg potassium; 139 mg caffeine (made with regular coffee); 63% calories from alcohol.

ICED CREME DE CACAO

This is an ideal ending to a cool, summer meal.

Serves: 2

Blend coffee with syrup and creme de cacao. Pour into two, ten-ounce stemmed glasses. Top with whipped cream, cocoa, and orange peel.

Each serving: 189 calories; 18 gm carbohydrate; trace protein; 5 gm fat (25% calories from fat); 17 mg cholesterol; 15 mg sodium; 150 mg potassium; 140 mg caffeine (made with regular coffee).

2 cups strong, cold coffee

2 teaspoons simple syrup (page 102)

2 ounces creme de cacao

2 tablespoons whipped cream, whipped

1/2 teaspoon cocoa powder

1/2 teaspoon grated orange peel

C OFFEE LIQUEUR

**1, 2-inch
vanilla bean**

**1 cup
cold water**

**1 cup dark
roast coffee**

1 cup vodka

**3/4 cup
brown sugar**

**1/4 cup
white sugar**

**2 tablespoons
dark molasses
(optional)**

Here's a delicious, homemade version of Kahlua. Although not as heavy as the commercial variety, our coffee liqueur is light and flavorful. For a heavier coffee liqueur, add dark molasses.

Serves: 16, 1-ounce servings

Place vanilla bean in coffee carafe. Brew coffee according to manufacturers' directions. (If coffee grounds will not fit in your filter basket, brew twice using half the coffee each time.) Allow coffee to cool. Brew through the grounds a second time.* Immediately add vodka, sugars and optional molasses. Pour into a clean, quart bottle with a tight-fitting stopper. Allow to cure for two days, then serve as Kahlua.

Each serving: 84 calories;11 gm carbohydrate; 0 gm protein; 0 gm fat (no calories from fat); 0 mg cholesterol; 12 mg sodium; 164 mg potassium; 140 mg caffeine (made with regular coffee); 46% calories from alcohol.

* After brewing coffee through the coffee maker, cool machine. Then clean as directed on page 25.

BIBLIOGRAPHY

Applegate, Liz. "What's brewin'?". RUNNER'S WORLD, November, 1989, page 22.

Anderson, Kenneth. THE POCKET GUIDE TO COFFEES AND TEAS. New York: G.P. Putnam and Sons, 1982.

Backus, Nancy. "Brew-ha-ha: good coffee sends guests away smiling." CONSUMER REPORTS, January 1991, page 31.

Barlow, Yvonne. "Espresso on the run." TRAVEL-HOLIDAY, February, 1989, page 100.

Billings, John David. HARDTACK AND COFFEE. Williamstown, Mass.: Corner House Publishers, 1973.

"...but on the other hand." SCIENCE NEWS, October 20, 1990, page 253.

Castle, Timothy J. THE PERFECT CUP Reading, Mass.: Addison-Wesley Publishing Co., 1991.

"Comeback time for coffee: let's have another cup and straighten this out." TIME, October 22, 1990, page 59.

COFFEE DRINKING SURVEY. London: International Coffee Organization, 1986.

Darroch, Nadina. COOKING WITH COFFEE. New York: Hart Publishing Co., 1978.

Davids, Kenneth. COFFEE. San Ramon, California: 101 Productions, 1987.

DeMers, John. THE COMMUNITY KITCHENS GUIDE TO GOURMET COFFEE. New York: Simon and Schuster, 1986.

Gordon, Jean. COFFEE: RECIPES, CUSTOMS, FACTS & FANCIES. Woodstock, Vt.: Red Rose Publications, 1963.

Ellis, Aytoun. THE PENNY UNIVERSITIES. London: Secker & Warburg, 1956.

"Fewer cups, but a much richer brew." BUSINESS WEEK, November 4, 1991, page 80. Grobee, Diederick et al. "Coffee, caffeine and cardiovascular disease in men." The New England Journal of Medicine, October 11, 1990, page 1026.

Ingall, Marjorie. "Now the good news about caffeine." MCCALL'S, August 1991, page 18.

Jacob, Heinrick Eduard. COFFEE: THE EPIC OF A COMMODITY. New York: Viking Press, 1935.

Kaufman, William I. *THE COFFEE COOKBOOK.* Garden City, New York: Doubleday & Company, 1964.

Kolpas, Norman. *THE COFFEE LOVERS' COMPANION.* New York: Quick Fox, 1977.

Kummer, Corby. "Before the first sip: how to start a good cup of coffee." *THE ATLANTIC,* May, 1990, page 117.

Kummer, Corby. "Untroubled brewing: ways to improve your coffee." *THE ATLANTIC,* June, 1990, page 107.

Knapp, Caroline. "Damn, that's a good coffee!" *MADEMOISELLE* February, 1991, page 62.

Lingle, Ted. *COFFEE CUPPERS' HANDBOOK.* Washington, D.C.: The Coffee Development Group, 1987.

Loud, Lance. "Coffee and Cigarettes." *AMERICAN FILM,* January 1990, page 16.

MacKay, Barbara. "What to drink when you exercise." *CHATELAINE,* June, 1989, page 38.

Oldenberg, Ray. *THE GREAT GOOD PLACE.* New York: Parragon House, 1989.

Mariani, John F. *AMERICA EATS OUT.* New York: Morrow, 1991.

McCoy, Elin and John Frederick Walker. *COFFEE AND TEA.* New York: New American Library, 1988.

Perry, Sara. *THE COMPLETE COFFEE BOOK.* San Francisco: Chronicle Books, 1991.

Reese, Diana. "Is coffee an aphrodisiac?" *NEW CHOICES FOR THE BEST YEARS,* September, 1990, page 30.

Rubin, Rita. "Good to the last drop? Coffee researchers spill the beans." *AMERICAN HEALTH,* September 1991, page 48.

Schwartz, Amy. *THE LADY WHO PUT SALT IN HER COFFEE.* San Diego: Harcourt Brace Jovanovich, 1989.

"Sex, seniors, and coffee-drinking habits." *SCIENCE NEWS,* February 3, 1990, page 78.

Shafer, Charles & Violet. *COFFEE.* San Francisco: Yerba Buena Press, 1976.

Smith, Emily T. "Coffee drinkers have no grounds for concern." *BUSINESS WEEK,* October 22, 1990, page 119.

The Specialty Coffee Association of America: One World Trade Center, Suite 800, Long Beach, California.

The Specialty Coffee Association of America: 1987 Tour to Costa Rica.

Stinchecum , Amanda Mayer. "Japan's other ritual: a coffee ceremony." *THE NEW YORK TIMES, November 17, 1991, section 5, page XX6.*

Svicarovich, John et al. *THE COFFEE BOOK. Englewood Cliffs, N.J.: Prentice Hall, Inc. 1976.*

"The Taste of Fresh-Brewed." CONSUMER REPORTS, January 1991, page 30.

Terrill, Ross. "The coffee house of Li Pingfen." *WORLD MONITOR, July 1989, page 34.*

Ukers, William. *THE ROMANCE OF COFFEE. New York: Tea and Coffee Trade Journal Co., 1948.*

Ward, Mary. Media Tour: "Brewing the Perfect Cup of Coffee." *Atlanta, Boston, Chicago, Cincinnati, Cleveland, Dallas, Detroit, Fresno, Houston, Los Angeles, Miami, Minneapolis, New York, Orlando, San Francisco, Seattle: Philips Home Products, Inc., 1987.*

Ward, Mary. Pamphlet: "How to Brew the Perfect Cup of Coffee." *Canton, Ohio: Philips Home Products, 1987.*

INDEX

Mary Ward has written other cookbooks,
including *The Hodgson Mill Oat Bran Cookbook,*
Blue Ribbon Breads with Carol Stine, and
Count Out Cholesterol Cookbook with Dr. Art Ulene.
She is a food stylist, nutrition consultant, and member of
the Specialty Coffee Association of America.
A wife, mother of three, and grandmother, she currently
resides in Cleveland, Ohio.